DOING GOOD

DOING GOOD

The Limits of Benevolence

Willard Gaylin

Ira Glasser

Steven Marcus

David J. Rothman

*With a new afterword by
David J. Rothman*

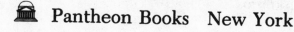 Pantheon Books   New York

Grateful acknowledgment is made to the following for
permission to reprint from previously published material:

The American Civil Liberties Union: Excerpts adapted
from "Life Under the New Feudalism" by Ira Glasser, *The
Civil Liberties Review* (Winter/Spring 1974). Copyright
© 1974 by The American Civil Liberties Union.
Reprinted by permission.
Harper's: Ira Glasser's article previously appeared in
slightly different form in the February 1975 issue of
Harper's Magazine. Copyright © 1975 by *Harper's
Magazine*. All rights reserved.
Alfred A. Knopf, Inc.: Adaptation of material from
Caring, by Willard Gaylin. Copyright © 1976 by Willard
Gaylin. Adapted by permission.

Library of Congress Cataloging in Publication Data
Main entry under title:
Doing good: the limits of benevolence.

   Includes bibliographical references.
   CONTENTS: Rothman, D., Introduction. —
Gaylin, W., In the beginning. —Marcus, S., Their
brothers' keepers. [etc.]
   1. Public welfare—Philosophy—Addresses, essays,
lectures. 2. Dependency (Psychology)—Addresses, essays,
lectures. 3. Benevolence—Addresses, essays, lectures.
4. Power (Social sciences)—Addresses, essays, lectures.
5. Public welfare—United States—Addresses, essays,
lectures. 6. Public welfare—Great Britain—Addresses,
essays, lectures.   I. Gaylin, Willard.
HV37.D44   1978   361   77—88776
ISBN 0—394—41133—1
ISBN 0—394—73372—X pbk.

Manufactured in the United States of America
NEW UPDATED EDITION
9

Acknowledgments

This project has received support and cooperation from many people and organizations, and it is a particular pleasure to acknowledge their roles. The New York Council for the Humanities, directed by Ronald Florence, together with the Center for Policy Research, directed by Amitai Etzioni, funded a conference and subsequent public discussions of dependency through a grant to David Rothman. Three public sessions were held: the first at Syracuse Universty, The Center on Human Policy, through the cooperation of Burton Blatt and Madeline Brager; the second took place at Adelphi University under the auspices of the University Programs on Aging and through the efforts of Elaine Goldman Jacks and Lilly Cohen; the final meeting was at the School of Social Work of the State University of New York at Buffalo under the coordination of Mary C. Schwartz and Isaac Alcabes. The tasks of administration at the Center for Policy Research were carried out with maximum efficiency by Stephanie Clohesy and Jolene Vrchota.

The essay by Ira Glasser owes much to the efforts and ideas of the author's colleagues at the New York Civil Liberties Union, who first challenged in court many of the assumptions examined in the essay.

That the project ultimately culminated in a book is in many ways due to André Schiffrin. He not only stimulated another series of debates among the authors but helped each of us to clarify and strengthen his arguments.

CONTENTS

INTRODUCTION

The origins of this book—the unusual process by which a psychoanalyst, a professor of comparative literature, a professor of history, and the director of the New York Civil Liberties Union came together to explore the theme of dependency—reflect not only networks of friendship and mutuality of interests, but some very novel assumptions and concerns in our political culture. The story begins (some will say, predictably enough) in the newly opened offices of a foundation, the New York Council for the Humanities. Its director, Dr. Ronald Florence, brought together a group of humanists (which we can simply define here as those in such fields as literature, history, and philosophy) with a group concerned with social policy (mostly litigators and administrators in public interest organizations) to offer suggestions as to how the council might promote a dialogue between the two. What would the humanities have to say about current concerns in social policy? What would those in social policy have to say that might affect the work of the humanists?

It was not very long into the meeting before the subject of poverty came up; remarks on Dickens and then Progressive America prompted remarks on the infant and the aged, and still others on foster children and the retarded. In short order we found ourselves talking about *the* dependent, asking who composed the category, what attributes they shared, how they differed. And the discussion did not stop there. Much more than definitional issues were at stake, for we were all very conscious—and not just because of the sponsorship of the meeting—of the matter of society's response to the dependent. Soon enough we found ourselves confronting what was to be the major theme that ran through one formal conference, several sessions with groups charged with day-to-day responsibility for the care of the dependent, and this book itself. Put succinctly, we recognized that a claim once considered to be of the most virtuous sort, the claim to be acting benevolently, had now become—to understate the point—suspect: if the last refuge of the scoundrel was once patriotism, it now appeared to be the activity of "doing good" for others, acting in the best interest of someone else.

That benevolence should appear to a surprisingly wide variety of observers to have devolved into mischievousness, that one wise and sensitive federal judge, upon hearing that we were going to investigate benevolence, could chide us for even considering seriously the idea that it was anything more than the exercise of power in disguise, is a very curious component in present-day intellectual and political perspectives. The humanists and those concerned with social policy were quickly and effectively joined around it. How was it that a concept of such traditionally high and noble standing, the text for countless ministers to preach on (Cotton Mather's *Bonifacius, An Essay Upon the Good,* kept running through my mind), was perceived as a positively dangerous impulse that ought to be curbed, maybe even eliminated? Could one construct and implement a humane and decent public policy toward the dependent without invoking, if not assuming, benevolent motives? If benevolence were ruled out, were we left with cruelty and neglect? Were we really prepared to say that the sins that could be committed in the name of doing good were the most grievous sins? For all the uneasiness that ran through this discussion, and despite our own discomfort in pursuing such matters, it was eminently clear (and would become still clearer as the inquiry progressed) that we were confronting one of the most important aspects of contemporary attitudes toward dependency. For better or worse, social thought and policy in our society seemed to be in the process of making a rather startling break with some very old and hallowed ideas.

In one sense, these essays represent an effort to demonstrate not only the feasibility but also the usefulness of joining the humanities with social policy. As it turned out, the scholars and the practitioners were able not just to talk to each other but also to hear each other. The opportunity to present and to debate the kinds of arguments that follow to people responsible for the care of the dependent young and old, the mentally ill, and the retarded was, I believe, significant to both sides. The presentations helped to place in a larger perspective many of the personal and institutional concerns that staff people had, concerns that they had believed were idiosyncratic. They did not just welcome the opportunity to debate the questions, they *needed* to debate them. The discourse was not a luxury, an interesting diversion, but an imperative, terribly pertinent to their everyday world. Issues that might be addressed in more abstract fashion—the rise of discretionary authority, the value of a paternalistic model in social policy—were rapidly translated into the more specific question: where should the authority of the caretaker leave off and the rights of the cared-for begin? In short, these sessions had an immediacy and a significance that none of us could have anticipated.

If nothing else, this dialogue on dependency reminded all of us involved that the humanities can bring a very special kind of rigor and relevance into the realm of social policy. This interdisciplinary approach will not usually resolve the issues; it certainly will not write the new code—but it will help to formulate the questions with a degree of clarity and precision that invariably improves chances for answers. We became acutely aware of the choices and the trade-offs that we are making.

In substantive terms, these essays are an attempt to clarify how it is that, particularly in the United States, dependency and benevolence have become such problematic subjects. Our predecessors may not have managed to resolve the problems of the poor or the aged or the orphan or the handicapped, but at least they did agree on the right direction for social policy to take. However great the gap between performance and goals, they shared first principles. More specifically, for most of this century, reformers, social activists, philanthropists—call them what you will—held firmly to the concept of the state as parent and to the desirability and efficacy of paternalistic interventions. There were those on the right of the political spectrum who insisted that the state ought to keep its hands off and not become intrusive; others to the left contended that only a revolutionary redistribution of power could ever resolve the problems of economic dependency. But the center held: the biological model of the caring parent that Willard Gaylin explores did structure social policy toward the dependent. Reform would come from the top down, from the better-off doing for the worse-off. The dependents could be cared for without any basic alteration in the social system.

But these assumptions are now under bitter attack. The very term "paternalism" has an unsavory quality, and so does the notion that the state should "play" parent. Gaylin, in analyzing these concepts, makes important distinctions, clarifying where paternalism does and does not make sense, and sets out the price that he believes we will pay (and it is a very heavy one) if we abandon such a model. But the very fact that he must vigorously defend the concept and tally the costs of ignoring it demonstrates that postulates once accepted as fundamental to social policy now appear to many observers to be of dubious value. The wisdom of the fathers seems, though perhaps mistakenly, wrongheaded to the sons.

From a Progressive way of looking at things, Steven Marcus and I are part of the problem, for both of us, using different periods of time and different types of data, set out to explore what has happened in the past in the name of benevolence. Marcus takes as his point of departure the operation of the "reforms" in English Poor Laws during the first part of the nineteenth century, particularly as they were perceived and criticized by such writers as Dickens and Wordsworth. My concern is with "reforms" promoted by the Progressives in twentieth century America; what happened as they brought a biological model of the caring parent into the political arena? Our efforts are not aimed at debunking, at stripping away reformers' credentials, but at analyzing the consequences of treating the state as though it were a parent. It may well be that Marcus and I create more problems than we solve, but Ira

Glasser's concluding essay is an effort to translate some of this perspective directly into an agenda for social policy. Glasser is frankly programmatic. In essence, he does not think that the needs and rights of the dependent need be in conflict, nor that to abandon paternalism is necessarily to breed neglect. He feels, and he is not alone in this, that we have finally begun to cut through rhetoric and unmask reality, so that now we can design a social policy that is decent and caring without being coercive.

Clearly there are tensions between the essays that are not altogether resolved. This is not a committee report in which we have tried to achieve a consensus around a set of recommendations. None of us has sacrificed a central point or even a casual aside for the sake of internal harmony. But just as clearly, there is a shared sense of values here: as the least common denominator, we are all four very self-consciously the children of Progressivism. We are repelled by the unfeeling neglect of the dependent, be it of the retarded at Willowbrook, the aged in corrupt nursing homes, the dependent young as they are shuttled from one inadequate setting to another, or the poor as they remain trapped in ghettos. I suspect that, as a result, there is a greater degree of agreement in this book than any of us would have predicted at the outset.

The very nature of that agreement opens us to a variety of attacks. Some may say that we are so busy tilting with our Progressive forebears that we fail to recognize just how much we resemble them. Their interventions may have been mischievous, but we are not yet prepared to abandon all interventions; they may have acutely abused the power of the state, but we are not prepared to eliminate the responsibilities of the state toward the dependent. In other words, we

are still part of an effort to resolve some of the problems of dependency that stops short of a total restruc-
turing of society. None of us is ready to await the
coming of the new age before we alter social policies
toward the dependent. Perhaps ours is an impossible
task; perhaps the dependent poor will never receive
their due until they hold political power themselves.
But that likelihood seems so far removed from the
realities we will confront in the foreseeable future that
we are ready to risk the charge that these are merely
stopgap measures or redressed liberal cant. For all the
possibility that we may be slaying one kind of do-
gooder only to substitute another, we believe the perspectives offered here do represent, modestly put, a
reformulation, or, more ambitiously, a fundamental
redefinition of the assumptions and practices that
guide social policy toward the dependent.

D.J.R.

New York City
August, 1977

IN THE BEGINNING:

HELPLESS AND DEPENDENT

Willard Gaylin, M.D.

IN A RECENT DISCUSSION BETWEEN SCIENTISTS AND theologians at an interdisciplinary conference on the "nature of man" (which could have been a replay of the Scopes trial), half of the group insisted on seeing *Homo sapiens* as one (albeit the highest) in a continuous line in the animal kingdom, while the other half of the group insisted on the uniqueness and special quality that separates the human being from all other creatures. Only this time the theologians, in defense of the rights of animals and nature, defined man as merely another animal variant; the scientists—while not quite speaking of "man in God's image"—implied as much with their equivalent terminology.

Coming from the traditions of science and medicine, I stand for man. *Homo sapiens* to me represents an incredible gap in "the great chain of life," a discontinuity that is not measurable in the traditional incremental changes from the lowest species of animal to the highest. We are a splendid and peculiar discontinuity—sui generis. And the irony in our development is that part of the uniqueness that makes us transcendent rests in the miserable, extended, helpless state in which we are born and remain for so long —untoward in the extreme, and unparalleled in the animal kingdom.

Looking at this period of early helplessness, we can see how it shapes our view of ourselves, and our future

3

attitudes toward the helpless of all categories: children, the aged, the sick, or the disadvantaged. Our capacity to identify, to feel compassion, to behave lovingly and charitably to the weak—when we are ourselves strong—will be determined in great part by the lessons we learned during our dependence.

Those outside the field have said that to psychoanalysts the first year of life is everything. Like most comments these days about psychoanalysis, this is an exaggeration. To a psychoanalyst like myself, the first year of life is *almost* everything. And that first year is controlled and dominated by one condition—the utter helplessness of the infant and his growing awareness of this dependent state.

In that masterpiece of his later years, *Inhibitions, Symptoms and Anxiety* (1926), Freud lists as one of the two most crucial factors in human development:

> the long period of time during which the young of the human species is in a condition of helplessness and dependence. Its intrauterine experience seems to be short compared to that of most animals, and it is sent into the world in less finished state. As a result the influence of the objective world upon it is intensified and it is obliged to make an early differentiation between the ego and the id. Moreover the dangers of the outer world have a greater importance for it, so that the value of the object which can alone protect it against them and take the place of its former intrauterine life is enormously enhanced. This biological factor, then, establishes the earliest situation of danger and creates the need to be loved which will accompany the child through the rest of its life.

"Dependency" is an ambiguous word with multiple meanings. Such words can create mischief unless we know specifically which definition we are attending to. One need only refer to the succeeding chapters of this volume to see how different professional biases and different frames of reference influence the way the word is applied, and even, at times, its very meanings. "Dependency" can refer to an actual state of being, whether physical or psychological; to an attitude and a self-evaluation; to a method of coping and adapting; to a description of relationship among people; to a mode of living, whether economic, sociological, or psychological; and more.

All these various meanings are interrelated, and all derive from a primal model, which I address here: the state of utter helplessness of human infants, and their total incapacity to survive without the ministrations of the adult members of the community. It is uniquely human, and so much a part of our existence and nature as to escape our detection.

The age of dependency and the borders of its duration are difficult to define. If one takes sexual maturity as the point of maturation, the human being spends roughly 20 percent of his life reaching that particular position, longer than any other species. Ironically, the cultural evolution of man has, if anything, aggravated the condition. While an individual is biologically capable of reproducing his own kind at puberty—anywhere from thirteen to fifteen years of age—he is incapable of assuming either the social or the economic role of the parent in our modern technological society. Thus we have extended and redefined the period of childhood even beyond the already extended biological base.

And if we take a period from birth to a point where we could readily expect the individual, if not the species, to survive (independent of the artifacts of cultural institutions of caring), *Homo sapiens* is even

more extreme in his period of helplessness. It is unlikely that a human child, dropped into a jungle setting, could find the means to its own survival before
the age of ten or twelve, or very close to the pubescent
period. So, in addition to the age of reproducibility of
kind, the age of autonomous functioning is also ex-
traordinarily delayed in human beings.

Finally, as if to intensify the unusually long period
of time in which the human child remains dependent,
the most singular aspect of human development is the
total helplessness of the human infant during this
early stage of his prolonged dependency. Adolf Portmann, the distinguished student of animal behavior,
has said:

> The most striking among those marks of our civilized
> state is the peculiarity of our early development. In-
> stead of continuing in the protection of the mother's
> body as long as would accord with our superior brain
> development, we are born as helpless creatures—in
> contrast to the state in which most mammals are born.
> Instead of beginning our life with self-developed limbs
> and the ability to move as freely as grown-ups of the
> species—like deer, calves, foals, like elephant cubs,
> young giraffes, whales, dolphins and seals—we have a
> special extrauterine first year very different from our
> further development, during which we gradually
> learn both to stand and to talk through social contact;
> we also learn purposeful action, the specific human
> fashion of controlling environment. None of these
> three facilities will be fully achieved if social contact
> is lacking or inferior. That is one of the reasons why
> biologists are eager to bring up both the correspon-
> dences and the differences between the behavior of
> man and of the animals most closely related to him.

Relatively uncomplicated and undifferentiated animals are capable of birth with a short gestation period,
and capable of participating in the struggle for sur-

vival soon after. A guppy must face life at the moment of birth. Autonomous and independent, it must avoid its first predator—its mother. More remarkably, a sea urchin is prepared to face a hostile environment only hours after the egg has been fertilized.

As one would expect, the more complicated the animal, the longer the gestation period, so that by the time we reach that relatively higher mammal, the elephant, we have a gestation period of twenty-two months. But, "It is a peculiarity of man that despite his higher level of differentiation he has to meet his environment far earlier than the elephant does."*

From the standpoint of the psychological development by which we identify human beings as such, beyond mere physiological and physical description, this dependency period is crucial—crucial, that is, in the development of a person who loves and is lovable, who has emotions and relationships, is capable of altruism and hope. For while all these attributes are biologically rooted, they will be psychologically encouraged or destroyed in the lessons of dependency learned in our peculiar period of extended helplessness.

Why is it, then, that man is born in such an utterly helpless state with practically no instinctual capacities for survival or self-preservation? As with many aspects of human uniqueness we turn to that remarkable instrument of evolution, the human brain. Given the nature of a human pelvis and the extraordinary size of the fetal brain at nine months, it is essential that the fetus pass through the birth canal at that time, even though this may mean that in comparison with other

*Adolph Portman, *Animals as Social Beings,* New York, Harper & Row, 1964, p. 126.

animals it is born with a peculiar and particular vulnerability.

This period of early infancy is the crucible and forge in which the potential of an animal is molded and shaped into the model of its kind—or damaged or destroyed. The neonate is "in process" in a way that the human being is at no other time of its postnatal existence.

Despite the fact that adults often know better intellectually, there is an inevitable emotional tendency to view the newborn infant as a miniature adult, at least on the physical level. But the newborn infant is no more a tiny adult physically than he is mentally or socially. He is an incomplete adult. Those adorable little wrists that are so appealing to doting parents are not wrists at all, but represent absences. The complete pattern of eight wrist bones will not be fully present until the child is close to five years of age. Similarly, crucial parts of the nervous system are not yet completed at birth. The child is incapable of performing certain activities because he simply does not have the equipment to do so. In addition, many of the developed parts of the neonate are present, but only in a state of extreme and delicate vulnerability, dependent on the proper environment in order to mature and develop; with an inappropriate environment they will atrophy and be destroyed.

For these reasons many authors have referred to the first year of life as a final stage of fetal life. This is merely a way of seeing gestation as having an intrauterine and an extrauterine period, comparable to the marsupials. Unlike the marsupials, however, there is no protective pouch—that "open uterus" to protect the fetus during this extrauterine gestation. Nor is there the automatic development enabled by the relatively constant and predictable environment of that pouch. Yet there must be some constant biological mechanism to protect so vulnerable a young. If there is no pouch, then the loving responses of the maternal organism must be its substitute. The newborn infant particularly requires specific treatments to thrive, because it is still in essence an extrauterine fetus undergoing rapid growth and development. If certain factors are withheld, it will die; withholding others will stunt physical development.

The various requisites for normal development can be collectively designated "nurture," and are dominated traditionally by the feeding situation. The child at the breast is the universal symbol of infancy. Freud termed this *orality,* or the oral stage, and his case for its primacy was so powerful that it dominated the literature in both psychoanalysis and child development until the 1950s. Psychoanalysts and learning theorists both conceived the primary bond between parent and infant as rooted almost exclusively in the feeding situation.

There is no question that the feeding process is the dominant event in both the biological existence of the child and its earliest psychological and social life. It is the primary factor in the communication between the infant and that person who, he quickly learns, supports his life-style as well as his life. There develops therefore a fusion—and confusion—between food and security that often lasts throughout life.

And feeding is more than the squirting of nutrients into a gastrointestinal tract, either in bottle or breastfeeding. While it is now fashionable to state that we are what we eat, what we eat in early life is predictable and relatively constant. The variable is actually the process and milieu of eating. It is a situation of embrace, pressure, contact, fondling, cooing, tickling, talking, stroking, squeezing; it is the warmth of the body, the pulsation of the parent's heart, the brushing of her lips, the smell of her secretions. This extended environment reinforces the child's fused image of security and food—and, at the same time, makes analysis of the feeding situation even more complex.

H. F. Harlow, the animal psychologist, in his now famous studies of the relationships of infant monkeys to artificial surrogates, divided the functions of mothering for a group of infant monkeys into two incomplete artificial mothers. One of them supplied nourishment in the sense of food, but was a cold, wired, nontactile feeding machine; at the same time there was present a warm, soft, terry-cloth "mother" which supplied no food nutrients at all. The studies demonstrated that the infant monkeys raised by these artificial surrogates invariably preferred (loved?) the warm and soft cloth mothers, despite the fact that they received no nourishment from them but got all of their life-sustaining food from the wire-mesh mother. It was with the terry-cloth mother that the infants chose to spend most of their time, clinging fiercely—possessive and desiring by every observable standard. Startling also was the fact that when exposed to any threat—an artificially created danger or potentially dangerous situation—it was to this terry-cloth mother that the infant monkeys retreated for reassurance.

In later studies, Harlow and some of his colleagues demonstrated the profound influence of withdrawing all social, tender, and loving contacts with one's own kind. They established experimental situations in which all the presumed ingredients for physiological development were supplied (nourishment, water, proper temperature, protection against diseases, etc.);

all that was missing was contact with a parent figure. In these studies the deprived creatures were almost unidentifiable as being "of their own kind" in terms of their social behavior. They had lost their "humanness" we would say if they were children. Anyone, regardless of how unsophisticated as to psychology or ethology, who has walked through a laboratory and seen some of these strange creatures, recognizes immediately something terribly disturbed in their attitudes. They indulge in odd, isolated, autistic behavior of the kind one sees in neglected, backward patients or the most severely retarded. They do not seem real or alive. These animals were raised with the cloth surrogate, which gives some contact comfort. While, as we have seen, this is better than the wire-mesh feeding machine, it is insufficient to guarantee the development of a normal adult. These conditions allow for the survival of the infant to adulthood, but produce an adult that cannot interrelate with its kind and cannot reproduce.

The studies showed further that the effect of isolation depended in great part on the time and duration of the contact deprivation. Up to three months of deprivation seemed in these animals to allow a certain reversibility; but animals isolated beyond that point, even for a period as short as six months, seemed permanently damaged.

The animals were deficient in precisely those features that are most closely associated in the human animal with his humanness: the capacity to enjoy the company of others, to relate socially and sexually, to become a member of a social unit, to have "emotions," to be able to play and to learn. It is difficult to isolate the specific deficiencies of the cloth surrogate, but obviously they relate to the whole complex interrelationship—the give and take of talk and touch, of feeding and fondling, of loving and caring—that produces infants who will later emerge into adults capable of assuming that same role with their own children.

Survival itself requires feeding, but feeding alone only guarantees the physical survival of "something," not necessarily a person. For the full development of a person, with sensitivities and sensibilities, with capacities to communicate and relate, a broader sense of nurture is necessary. It is necessary to care for a child in a specifically "loving" way in order to initiate a similar capacity in the child.

While this prolonged early helplessness demands much from the parent, it also imposes a new set of rules in the relationship of the individual to his developing society. No other helpless animal in its infancy is endowed with so much awareness. As the human child develops, he soon becomes cognizant of his utter helplessness and his dependence on those around him, and their goodwill, for his survival. If gestation is considered to extend through the year beyond birth, it is a peculiar kind of gestation, for it is the gestation of an *aware* fetus who, while helpless to act, is not helpless to perceive, and with that perception is learning lessons he will never forget.

One would think, therefore, that dependency would have played a central role in any psychoanalytic theory of human development, but it has not. How is it that such a factor, so closely linked to the biological nature of the species—to the very survival of that species—could be so ignored? The answer lies in a further paradox: even survival is a peripheral and neglected concept in traditional, early psychoanalytic literature. The explanation for this lies in the peculiar history of the psychoanalytic movement in general, so dominated by the genius and personality of Freud.

It is not that Freud failed to recognize the central nature of the dependent state. In his writings in applied psychoanalysis Freud repeatedly alluded to the impact of the early state of helplessness, as, for example, in *Civilization and Its Discontents* (1930), where he clearly traced man's need for religion back to that original feeling of infantile helplessness. But in the central body of his psychoanalytic thought, whose primary concern, after all, was in developing the theory of neurosis, the sexual instinct and its vicissitudes dominate the discussion of the nature of man to an overwhelming degree. Here is the libido theory on which all modern psychoanalysis was based: an instinctual theory, which essentially attempts to explain all development in terms of a person's internal conflict rather than in terms of that person's relationships. Of course Freud acknowledged that both sets of conditions existed, but the focus of his theoretical work was on the internalized struggle and the constitutional nature of human behavior. This choice of emphasis was to have an enormously enriching effect on Freudian theory. It permitted him—indeed, forced him—to study human development. It allowed psychoanalysis to become more than a limited tool for the treatment of restricted emotional disorders, permitting its development into a potent psychological explanation of normal human behavior.

On the other hand, this frame of reference did tend to take man out of his milieu, and it led to the neglect of crucial aspects of human behavior, such as identification and dependency. Starting in 1905 with the publication of *Three Essays on the Theory of Sexuality*, the global model under which more technical theories developed was that of an instinctually (sexually) driven animal, in which conflicts with the environment precipitated defensive maneuvers; but neurosis arose from the internal struggles of "man against himself."

The external conflicts with the environment were reserved as the focus for Freud's work in applied, rather than theoretical, psychoanalysis, outside the medical model, where his interest was directed to culture, religion, and other institutions of social living. Here, too, however, the instinct theory dominates. The instinct seeks for the gratification of release; in his drive for instinctual pleasure, the individual comes in conflict with an often inhibiting and frustrating environment; the problem for the individual is to bring his drives under the control of a reality principle that necessitates either the frustration, inhibition, sublimation, or modification of those drives to meet the standards of the civilized world. This thesis reached its culmination in a book that was to have a profound effect on sociologists and political scientists—*Civilization and Its Discontents.* Here the essential image is that of an individual striving for gratification of (at this point) both aggressive and sexual drives, who is kept under control by the forces of civilization. This view of *Homo sapiens* depicts him as essentially individualistic and selfish, with civilization as the restraining force keeping him in check.

The concept of individualism, which was born and thrived in the nineteenth century (particularly in America), was to achieve even further idealization in the twentieth century. But man is not, technically speaking, an individual; a social structure is a part of his biology and a necessary part of his functioning: we are a social animal not by election but by nature. Precisely because of our prolonged dependency, we could not survive as a species or develop as a type were there not a social structure to support us. While man is not quite a colonial animal like coral, he is certainly also not a true individual like an amoeba. He rests somewhere in between, and no theory of the nature of man is complete that does not recognize the obligate social structure in which he must develop. It is to an earlier work of Freud's, *Totem and Taboo,* that we must turn to find his acknowledgment of this.

Totem and Taboo was Freud's first attempt to analyze social structure and its relation to human nature. Ironically, the message is quite different from—indeed, almost antithetical to—that of *Civilization and Its Discontents.* Freud was interested at this time in examining the incest barrier in particular, but also the origins of certain religious rituals and taboos. This, then, is his first detailed study of organized morality. It draws heavily on Darwin's "primal horde" theory of the origin of society, but also on Atkinson's *Theory of Social Origin* derived from a study of ape populations.

Freud postulated a "scientific myth" that man once existed in a primal horde, and he assumed that understanding the conditions of that existence might help to explain the evolution of certain moral principles. This primal horde—with father, mother, and children—became disrupted when the younger male members (brothers) clamored for sexual access to the females (mothers and sisters) in the clan. This eventually led, Freud postulates, to a revolt by the brothers; patricide; the eating of the father; and the reinstitution of male-dominant clans. But now, with the knowledge of their inception clearly in mind, a sense of instability and fear was introduced that could destroy the base for social life. The succeeding generation, with a sense of guilt and horror, recognizes that the same thing might happen to them. The totemic taboos that prohibit killing of the totemic animal (symbol of the father) and the abolition of incest would be seen then to be partly an act of obedience after the fact, a mechanism to handle guilt, and partly a recognition that order was necessary for the survival of all. "The incest barrier probably belongs to the historical acquisitions of humanity and like other moral taboos it must be fixed in many individuals through organic heredity." Freud, under the influence of Jung at this time, postulates that we have inherited the memories of that early primal horde situation, and that through this inheritance we have established certain moral taboos and restrictions on behavior which will allow for civilized living.

We know that we cannot genetically *inherit* memory traces from an ancestral past. But the actual mechanism is unimportant. Even the theory of the primal horde itself is unimportant. If one strips *Totem and Taboo* of these two specifics, the message becomes clear: certain revulsions, certain moral behavior patterns, are so essential for the survival of the species that they cannot be accidents of culture but must be built into the genetic nature of the species. To think otherwise, to shift certain moral behavior exclusively into the cultural area, is to make the survival of the species the luckiest of all accidents—and Freud no longer believed in "accidents."

What Freud has said about the incest taboo may or may not be true, but certainly something similar to it must be true about the protective, loving, caring attitudes of the adult human being toward the child. Given the prolonged dependency period of human beings, it is unlikely that the protective response of the adult for the young would not be part of the genetic inheritance.

Survival tends to be visualized in most systems today in terms of "fight or flight"—and the physiological underpinnings that support those two great adaptive maneuvers. But the human infant is capable neither of fleeing nor of fighting. The infant does not see his survival in avoiding the source of danger, which he does not even recognize, and surely not in overcoming the danger, which inevitably is beyond his limited coping capacities. The first—and for a long time, the only—method of survival is neither fight nor flight, but rather something that might be called clutch or cling.

It is impossible, of course, directly to establish the thinking of an infant; yet it is a worthwhile speculation, which many have attempted. Once one strips away the technical language from the essential substantive thought, there is a remarkable similarity in all the varying theories of developmental psychology that presume a consciousness and a cognition.

The earliest stage of childhood development has been described variously as primary narcissism or magical omnipotency. But basic to most views of this period is an image of an infant who is aware of self and probably unaware of environment. This earliest stage is dominated by the child's sensations—not yet necessarily even emotions. He senses needs, pains, hunger, discomfort, pinpricks, wetness, and so on. What is meant when we say the child is feeling hunger? Certainly the "concept" of hunger in the first days of life is unknown to him. What he is aware of is pain due to gastrointestinal activity or even, possibly, to some psychic extension of that. He screams (rage?), and seemingly his scream produces—in time—a warm suffusion of liquid into the gastrointestinal tract, relieving the distress. The child is not aware of a complicated sequence of events that transpires between the scream and the alleviation of his distress. He cannot possibly know that the cry may awaken a somnolent parent who may then go through the detailed business of warming a bottle or preparing for nursing, and so on. The child does not interpret his own cry as a call for attention or a plea for help. At this stage of his development, if any conceptualization is possible, it is that the cry *itself* produces the satisfaction desired. This sense of self alone, and in control of the satisfaction of one's needs, is called magical omnipotence.

When the child begins to sense environmental factors, he will likely at first egocentrically identify them as extensions of himself. Only gradually will the child become aware of the environment around him as a distinct entity—and how his concept of self then changes! He becomes aware that not only is he not magically omnipotent, he is not even potent. He is totally powerless, incapable of ensuring any of his creature comforts, let alone the essential needs of his survival. With a fall that must rival the fall of the angels (perhaps inspiring that myth?), he is reduced from the highest of creatures to the lowest.

But this awareness is mitigated in turn by the recognition of other figures in that environment who are strong and who care. The first differentiated figure is unquestionably the parent; and while the child's sense of himself diminishes, his sense of the parent's full powers is magnified. The capacities of the parent are more than adequate to attend the infant's limited needs for almost total satisfaction. The child then enters a stage of delegated omnipotence, overvaluing the parental figures and seeing them now in the role in which he had formerly cast himself. There are, indeed, awesome, powerful figures who occupy the universe. They may not be the child itself, but by some glorious happenstance they are capable of supplying him with all that he needs.

With time he will begin to learn that these parental figures not only have the power to give pleasure, to support needs, to satisfy desires, but also the power to withhold. Ironically, it is in the recognition of the parents' discriminatory capacity, rather than of their automatic giving, that the child will begin to sense his own power. He will begin to see that he too has, if not direct, at least a derivative power via his influence with the adult figure. It is not just that the parents have the capacity to supply his needs; he now has the more sophisticated knowledge that they are *willing* to supply his needs just as they are capable and willing to love. Awareness thus begins to build the mechanism that links dependency through love to survival. To be helpless is not necessarily to be in jeopardy. To be helpless *and unloved* is the matrix of disaster. The "power" of helplessness fuses with the "power" of lovability to become an essential part of the complicated dependency lessons that the infant will almost inevitably carry into his adult life.

This loving and caring capacity is obviously a complex one. It may be limited in some individuals, as there are parents who beat, destroy, or simply do not tend to their children. What is crucial is the degree to which this capacity is limited. If the deprivation is sufficiently severe, either the survival of the small human being, or the nature of his humanity, will be imperiled. But these occasional abnormalities cannot gainsay the inclination to caring that is an essential part of the nature of our species. The evidence for parental caring can be derived deductively from the fact that the greatest sacrifice demanded of a parent is traditionally not that person's own life, which sacrifice is entered into willingly in many cultures, but the sacrifice of his or her child. When God wished to test Abraham, it was the sacrifice of Isaac that was demanded; the horrible price that Artemis demanded of Agamemnon was the death of Iphigenia; and, finally, the only offering sufficient to demonstrate the extent of God's love of man was the sacrifice of His Son.

We are caring people, despite the fact that it may be fashionable now to deny it. How much of our capacity to care may have been damaged by our culture remains to be seen, but that some is left is observable in the everyday behavior of human beings as well as in biology and literature. We respond not only to the child, but to the childlike; we respond to the helpless, whether animal or human. All forms that have an infantile representation are particularly capable of touching us. Witness the current campaign to preserve the harp seal, which inevitably features pictures of this plump, sad-eyed, soft, and cuddly creature. While bearing a certain sympathy for endangered species, I nonetheless ask you to consider that if the species endangered had the same name but a different form, would the campaign have been as effective? Supposing the young harp seal was a thirty-pound animal that looked like a giant cockroach or beetle. Would we have responded to the pathetic plight of this "baby" if visualized, full-blown in The New York Times, with his beady eyes, hard shell, crawling antennae, and overenlarged incisors? I suspect not. We are subject to an aesthetic bias that is very much related to the natural tendency to care for the young and to visualize any young in terms of *our* young. It is difficult to perform controlled experiments, but subjective evidence is at hand that the pug-nosed, blue-eyed, freckle-faced prototypic choirboy transgressor of the law inevitably will be judged in a different perspective from the pimply-faced, obese, and unattractive child of the same age. We respond to a certain visual image (baby-faced?) that may go back to biological derivations. Certain features, prepubescent and soft, relate in our minds to innocence, and ultimately to helplessness; and it is the helplessness of the child that in all probability evokes protective response in the normal adult.

It is important to realize that the human being is the *least* instinctually fixed animal on earth. It is testament to man's power, authority, and uniqueness that even nature only dares *suggest* to him future courses of action which he may then choose to embrace or ignore. So it is quite possible in the course of our development that many of us will obliterate even our response to helplessness and become desensitized to this as we are capable of desensitizing ourselves to other aspects of our personal potential. But there is ample evidence of a readiness, on an intuitive and almost reflexive pattern, to respond to the helpless of our species.

Similarly, I am absolutely convinced that there is a contagious quality to tears. If a grown man would uncontrollably begin to shed tears in front of a group of strangers, a choked reaction would be elicited in a number of them independently of the knowledge of what caused the tears.

The capacity to respond to the visual image of the helplessness of others may well explain, among other factors equally important, the public response to the death of the Kennedy brothers and Martin Luther King, Jr. The fact that we were capable of visualizing via the medium of television the distress of those

around them added a greater reality and fuller identification with their tragedy. It is inconceivable to me
that anyone, independent of political judgment or position, could have witnessed Senator Edward
Kennedy's eulogy for his brother and, at the moment
at which he seemed to lose control, when his voice
began to break, not find a welling of his own grief.

Symbols of separation have often been used as a
visualization of the most dreaded fates of men,
whether it be in banishment from country or isolation
from kind, Ulysses the wanderer or Leopold Bloom
("the only Jew in Ireland"), the Flying Dutchman or
Ishmael: the person detached or separated from his
loved ones, his protectors, his home, or his kind is a
tragic figure. Such separation is visualized as a fate
comparable to death. Indeed, it may be that the principal way the human being is ultimately capable of
visualizing death is via separation. For death is so ter-
rible an absence that we tend to deny its existence.
Since we are incapable of perceiving something without ourselves as the perceiving agent, we often see
death not as the absence of us, but as the absence of
everything except us. It is the horrifying dream of
being buried alive.

This general equation, set early in childhood, of isolation (more exactly abandonment) with death makes
our current traditional treatment of the dying particularly insensitive, cruel, and damaging. For a multitude
of reasons—perhaps not the least important being our
own massive need to deny death—we tend to treat the
dying as though they were already dead. We isolate
them, under the pretext of giving them adequate
medical care, but in reality to protect ourselves from
them. They are the painful reminders of an inevitable
future we attempt to deny. It may even be that our

extension of puritanical attitudes which demand that we sustain life to the absolute, even while withholding the drugs that make terminal existence bearable, bespeaks in itself a punitive attitude toward the dying. Certainly, it too reveals our readiness to deny death, even at the cost of adding anguish to the process of dying.

Certainly the *child* is more threatened by withdrawal of love than by the foolish parent who might threaten to kill him. While death psychologically probably does not exist even for the adult, it most certainly does not exist for the young child. The withdrawal of love is close enough, and as such is a greater coercive force.

Somewhere behind all of this, we must know that death is a process and a procedure in which we will all participate some day. If we can nonetheless suspend our normal compassions to this group in which we all will achieve membership, it is not surprising that we can suspend compassion from the powerless when we have assured power, from the poor when we have secure wealth, and from the dependent when we have established independence.

Beyond direct observation of the child, indeed preceding it, certain assumptions about childhood perceptions were made by psychoanalysts who observed both the unconscious fantasies of patients and, specifically, neurotic behavior. It is the assumption of psychoanalysis that an individual lives in a world of his own perception, deviating from such actuality as may exist through the distortion imposed by his own personal experience. Our past is the lens through which we observe the present. In the symptoms of neurosis, one sees an actual regression of behavior into the protective illusions of the past. If one examines an obsessional neurosis, or simply the obsessional behavior in which most of us indulge from time to time, it is amazing how much it relates to the rewarded behaviors of childhood. We tend to be obsessive about cleanliness, bowel habits, straightening, tidying, and waking and bedding activities. In the obsessive's behavior we so often see those qualities that were deemed "good" in the child by parental standards.

A similar link to childhood definitions of security through dependence can be extrapolated by examining phobic behavior. At one time it was thought each individual phobia had a distinct interpretation; fear of heights always meant x and fear of crowds, y. We now see more clearly the common thread that binds these diverse symptoms into a consistent pattern. Many phobias seem to involve the concept of entrapment: elevators, subways, tunnels, airplanes, bridges, situations in which there seems no way out. When one examines such situations, they seem at first to imply danger, but to many of these patients it is also the sense of "no way out," or, more precisely, "no way home." If anxiety is first felt in relation to the environment in the early days of life, it is surely not the castration anxiety that dominates much of later life, but separation anxiety. The phobic can be seen, across the specific symbols of an overdetermined symptom, to share this common terror of separation from home, a terror distressingly similar to that pictured in its extreme on the face of a two-year-old momentarily separated from his parent in a crowd. Safety here is visualized, if not in the parents, at least in the tangible symbolic aspects residual in them. The individual who despairs of his own capacity for coping regresses to the earliest mechanism of adaptation—dependency. He recalls a time when he was safe because he was loved.

Even the briefest memory of caring in the early stages of life may be used to build an illusion of safety.

When we move from the simple paradigm of healthy mother and healthy child into extensions of dependency that are more complicated, we must be careful to modify our generalizations and to reexamine our moral premises. There is always danger in taking a biological paradigm as a basis for ethical behavior.

The prolonged period of early dependency that all of us as human creatures experience is—despite its abject and ludicrous impotence—a testament to our future potential power. Even as one watches the clinging, sucking, attaching, fusing mechanisms of the child, one sees, interlaced with them, the gropings away from the parent into the outside world, the excitement of discovering autonomy and the freedom implicit in it, and the confusion between clinging and venturing that is so evident in the world of the one- and two-year-old. Dependency is intended to be outgrown. It is a device to facilitate its own end in the creation of the mature and independent adult.

There are stages in life, however, in which we will once again be reduced to states of dependency for temporary periods, or even permanently. There are as well people who, because of accident of condition, will never reach independence.

In discussing dependency on a broader social level I refer here neither to the metaphoric or poetic sense in which we are all interdependent, nor to such elegant extensions of the concept as in the sensual dependence on beautiful things of the aesthetically inclined, or the decadent dependence of the wealthy on their servants. I am using the word dependency here in its most manifest sense, as the state of people who are "unable to exist or function satisfactorily without the aid or use of another."

Using survival at its most basic creature level, there are a number of individuals who will never achieve a state of independence, or will do so only in relatively fragmented or limited aspects of their lives. One thinks of the severely handicapped child—the severely retarded, the severely crippled, the autistic child. These are groups then who will be maintained within certain, if not all, aspects of the dependency situation for their entire lives. Some may reach intellectual independence; some may even reach economic and social independence (while never reaching physical or physiological independence); some—the most severely damaged—will remain in a totally infantile stage for their entire lives. Disease, aging, and trauma will also increase the ranks of the dependent.

To talk of the nature of things, of course, is not to judge the rightness of them. Biologists have been accused of being "natural law" philosophers in the most simplistic sense of that term. There is a tendency, when emerging from the tradition of biology and medicine, to define the "good" in terms of the "normal." It is "normal" to have a blood pressure within a certain range, therefore it is healthy—a medical term for "good"—to have such a blood pressure.

When I discuss, therefore, the natural order of things, the state of dependency that must exist, and the caring nature that must be present organically in the structure of human beings to facilitate the development of the species, I am saying that this parentalism and caring, this nature of *Homo sapiens,* is good not because it is normal but because it is necessary for the survival of the species, and because I visualize "goodness" as being the burden of that specific species. Perhaps what I am saying then is closer to the

"Agere sequitur esse"—the ought is founded in the is.

But what is the *esse* in human nature? Part of the wonder of that nature is that what we are is in great part up to us. In a medieval Talmudic text, the question was raised, "If God had intended man to be circumcised, why would he have not created him in such form?" And the answer that was given had a wisdom that transcends the specificity of the question: "Man, alone amongst animals, is created incomplete but with the capacity to complete himself." We are the executors of our future. Our current sense of self is the God in whose image future man will be created.

The fact that something is, therefore, does not mean that it ought to be so. When we enter into sociological or economic discussions of dependent populations, such as those of Marcus, Rothman, and Glasser, caution must be exercised in the lessons we draw from that biological model. It is essential to be aware of the degree to which we may trust the observations from this primal paradigm and to what degree we can predict the variabilities that will issue from changing the nature of the caretaker, the nature of the cared for, and the quality of the contract between them.

We see the complications in, for example, the problem of delegating consent to a next of kin. Rooted in our family-oriented society is a sense of the congruence of interest between the normal parent and the child. The helpless child, of course, cannot speak for himself, and we must trust that identity of interest bound in nature that generally insures the compassionate concern of the parent for child. We grant, therefore, great power in this relationship not just because the child is the ultimate responsibility of the parent but because we are inclined to trust the general concern of the parent.

It is obvious, however, that the relation of a mother

to a child may differ from that of the father and will surely differ from that of the brother or sister or aunt or uncle or second cousin once removed. As we move farther and farther away from our original paradigm we rightfully trust less the natural bonds of affection that tie the caretaker to the dependent. We are more inclined to legalistically hedge the power of the surrogate, and we would be wise to assume an increasing divergence between the interests of the helpless and the self-interest of the strong. The parent of a healthy six-month-old child simply does not bear the same relation to that child that an estranged son-in-law does to the senile, wealthy old lady to whom he is the next of kin.

When we move farther from the concept of next of kin to vesting authority in a social or political institution, our original paradigm becomes stretched quite thin. No social institution, regardless of how benevolent or paternalistic, can ever replicate the parent-to-child symbiosis. While individuals within institutions —nurses, attendants, physicians, and the like—may demonstrably exercise affection, tenderness, caring, even love, the power of authority is vested for the most part within the abstract concept of "the institution," and the intuitive responses of biology undergo strange transmutations in the structural organization of bureaucracies.

The model varies in a different way when the change is not with the caretaker but in the dependent. The normal mother herself may not respond with the same intuitive caring to a crippled or deformed child as she would to a healthy one. She may be so threatened, guilty, or simply repelled that those caring attitudes that intuitively are designed to insure the survival of the species will not be elicited. It may well be that the natural revulsion toward the deformed is it-self a reflection of the utilitarian nature of our species, which, driven by a Darwinian need to guarantee sur-vival of the fittest, has built-in mechanisms to insure that only the healthy elicit the nurturing responses of the parent. Also, the relationship of the mother to the institutionalized child will be quite different from her relationship to the child raised in her home; similarly with the abnormal child and the healthy one; the child of twenty and the newborn.

In all of the examples that I offer, I start with the basic assumption of a definition of dependency, using for models the physically and mentally incompetent. Another chapter will deal with the concept of "the dependent poor." I exclude from my discussion this group not simply because my roots are in biology and medicine, but also because I feel that there are crucial distinctions in the uses of the word dependency, and that the model I originally offered may be dangerous, even in analogy, when extended to other areas. For purposes of our discussion, then, I think it is impera-tive to separate the two groups of dependent popula-tions one finds in our culture. For want of any tradi-tional term, I will define one as the intrinsically dependent and the other as the extrinsically depen-dent.

The intrinsically dependent are those cited; so physically, mentally, or emotionally handicapped that they are incapable of taking care of themselves, such as some of the mentally ill, mentally retarded, crip-pled, or senile. The second group, the extrinsically dependent, are those I define as individuals made de-pendent by artifacts of our culture. They have the intrinsic capacity for mature and autonomous func-tioning, but because of social or economic roles are in positions where they are incapable of supporting themselves at the most fundamental level. This group would include the poor, certain of the elderly, women constricted by cultural definitions, and even some groups whose dependence seems so logical and inevitably part of their lives that we do not recognize it as an artifact, such as the dependent adolescent. As a biologist and psychologist, I suggest such economic uses of dependency as are dealt with so poignantly in Steven Marcus's chapter are not only arbitrary and unnecessary but harmful; I therefore reject the term dependency for the poor, and I caution the sociologist, political scientist, and economist against such usage. It is an indignity for an adult who has no intrinsic needs for care and maintenance to be reduced to the level of a child—with all the concomitant humiliations— because of a social system that deprives him of the rites of passage into maturity. We have seen how love, kindness, and caring first require self-pride and self-love. It is crucial that one who is capable be allowed to see oneself as adult. If we can find ways to eliminate the category of the extrinsically dependent, it is we who will benefit.

Whenever a person's sense of control over his own life is expanded; whenever he sees himself as the source of his own pleasures and security, his pride increases, his self-esteem increases, and his capacity for caring and concern is enhanced with it. The opportunity to sense one's self as a competent, independent, coping person allows one the generosity, unavailable in the humiliation of dependence, of sharing one's self with others and of exposing one's self to the vulnerability that loving inevitably implies. When an individual can be more self-reliant, fewer of his relationships have to be centered around the rather unreciprocal fulfillment of his own personal needs. He can proceed to service, to participation, to self-sacrifice, to love, to creativity, and to the caring for the intrinsically help-less.

To me, then, there is no profound problem in the care of the extrinsically dependent. The solution is simply to alter the category. And it is "merely" a tech-nological problem. Those of you versed in the eco-nomic and political mechanisms must come up with a solution.

The question remains, however, not how, but in what ways we are deficient in our ministrations to those who are intrinsically dependent, as in the exam-ples of the institutionalized child and the helpless el-derly. The elderly represent a peculiar group, which should demand our attention if only because they form a constituency to which all of us (unless relieved by a premature death) will eventually belong. They are our future and our destiny, and one is usually most careful with those things with which one can readily identify. Perhaps that is part of the answer. In a youth-oriented culture such as ours we do not identify with the aged because we do not intend to ever become old. Plastic surgery, artificial body parts, cosmetics, life-style, self-deception, will keep us, we narcissisti-cally believe, Peter Pans.

There are, however, other indices of the lack of compassion for those of limited power; of the bullying of the weak by the strong. How can I explain this while defending the genetic directive for caring as basic to our species? How do I explain the alienation that per-mits the kind of street brutality that is an everyday occurrence in our lives? What is the linkage between dependency, loving, caring, and their antonyms? Why are we finding it difficult to extend a natural paternal-

istic concern to the helpless and disadvantaged who
share our time and space?

It is fashionable these days to view paternalism and
benevolence as obscene terms. The reformers of the
past are often ridiculed for failures to achieve their
ends. Worse, their intentions are suggested to be motivated by unconscious self-serving. "Unconscious motives" are dirty words best left to the privacy of the
psychoanalytic retreat. Judge not that ye be not
judged. I have little faith in the eventual success of the
best-intended of our current laborers in their efforts
for equity and justice. Still I revere their intentions
and their effort.

There will always be the need for parental compassion; at the same time, there will always be the need
for vigilance in recognizing the limitations of institutions of government as surrogate parents. Nonetheless
it is not parentalism that is the crime, it is what is
passed off for parentalism. The language of rights,
with its litigious and paranoid assumption that good
can only be received from others by pursuit and protection of law, must also recognize that the good that
can be received from others in that way is often quite
limited. We cannot, for example, "coerce" a parent
into caring for a child. We may withdraw the child
from the uncaring parent, but unless we can find a
"paternalistic" alternate parent, the child will be little
benefited by our intrusions. Certain minimal rights
ought to be defended even beyond the court—in the
streets if necessary; but the solution to our problems
will require that we go beyond the kind of moral behavior that can be defined in terms of plaintiff and
litigant. The Supreme Court decision on racial inte-
gration in the schools did not solve the problem, nor
will converting the country into a convoy of armored

buses. Court decisions are often essential steps, but we must recognize that they are only steps and that something else will also be required. Those factors in our more basic cultural institutions that link us as brothers and sisters, in the image of parent to child, are not mere sophistry, but an essential for a just society. Rights morality will never supplant concepts of responsibility, moral duty, and obligations to care.

Caring—that is, the protective, parental, tender aspects of loving—is a part of relationship among peers, child to parent, friend to friend, lover to lover, person to animal. The parent-child aspect of caring is only the essential paradigm whose presence is necessary for the diffusion of this human quality into the other relational aspects of life. The linkages between being cared for and caring for others are crucial to remember.

Even with severe deprivations something of the child will survive. How "human" that something will be will, to a tremendous extent, depend on the nature of the nurture provided to the developing human being. As light and visual stimulation are essential for the development of the capacity to see, so to be cared for is essential for the capacity to be caring.

To be totally unaccepted, to be totally unloved—indeed, to be almost totally disapproved—either requires the rejection of one's self (an intolerable situation) or a total dissociation from the judging individual. Such total dissociation is dangerous, however, when we are required to live in a social community. Surely the kind of adolescent brutality that is evidenced in the newspapers every day, in which a street mugger hits a random woman over the head with a lead pipe as a convenient means of gaining the $6 in her purse, implies more than just the need for $6. It suggests that the concept of identity has been destroyed, or never developed; that the person now feels so "other" that he is no longer within the framework of identification necessary for introjection of a value system. Such behavior is beyond the golden rule, for that implies the identity of personhood between the other and you. Obviously, it is more analogous to the squashing of a bug approaching your picnic table. To give up on one's self is to give up on one's own personal value, and ultimately to give up on a sense of values.

If we are not cared for by others, we cannot care for ourselves. A society that treats any serious segment of its population—whether blacks, women, or youth—with distaste or disrespect runs the risk of convincing that group of its own inadequacy and thus alienating it from identification with the group and allegiance of its moral codes. If we do not care for ourselves, we cannot care for others. Giuseppe Mazzini said that "we improve with the improvement of humanity; nor without the improvement of the whole can you hope that your own moral and material condition will improve. Generally speaking, you cannot, even if you would separate your life from that of humanity; you live in it, by it, for it." We must all trust ourselves and love ourselves for the primary purpose of loving others and caring for them. This extends beyond the world of the child and into the life of the adult. We do not choose to live in social relations; we are obliged to. It is this obligation to live in groups that renders the destruction of social living so dangerous, and makes a neglect of the problems of public safety by the social and behavioral scientists so distressing.

When we neglect the weak and helpless, the disenfranchised and disadvantaged, we betray our loving nature and endanger the social future that depends on our caring. All of us, after all, inevitably spend our lives evolving from an initial to a final stage of dependency. If we are fortunate enough to achieve power and relative independence along the way it is a transient and passing glory, and it would be well to keep clearly in mind our inevitable decline as we contract and deal with the helpless and dependent who come within our influence.

Further, our only demonstrable immortality resides in our progeny. The social institutions we build will determine the kind of world we deed our children. It will determine their potential for survival—and therefore our own. So we must design these institutions with care and concern rather than with the arrogance of ephemeral power. When the rich ignore the needy and the strong exploit the weak, the powerful are themselves diminished. When we alienate a group of our population, when we deprive them of whatever those resources are that build dignity and compassion, we are in time destroying ourselves. The unity of man is no romantic myth. It is a biological fact that we ignore with peril.

FURTHER READING

Ainsworth, M. D. S. "Attachment and Dependency: A Review." In J. L. Gewirtz (ed.), *Attachment and Dependency*. Washington, D.C.: V. H. Winston, 1972.

———. "The Development of Infant-Mother Interaction Among the Ganda." In B. M. Foss (ed.), *Determinants of Infant Behavior,* vol 2. New York: Wiley, 1963.

———. "Object Relations, Dependency and Attachment: A Theoretical Review of the Infant-Mother Relationship." *Child Development* 40 (1969), pp. 969–1025.

Bowlby, J. *Attachment and Loss,* vol. 1: *Attachment.* New York: Basic Books, 1969.

———. *Attachment and Loss,* vol. 2: *Separation: Anxiety and Anger.* New York: Basic Books, 1973.

———. "The Nature of a Child's Tie to its Mother." *International Journal of Psychoanalysis* 39 (1958), pp. 350–73.

Brazelton, T. B., School, M. L., and Robey, J. S. "Visual Responses in the Newborn." *Pediatrics* 37 (1966), pp. 284–90.

Dobzhansky, Theodosius. *Mankind Evolving.* New Haven: Yale University Press, 1962.

Dubos, René. *Man Adapting.* New Haven: Yale University Press, 1965.

Freud, S. *Civilization and its Discontents,* 1930. Standard edition, vol. 21. London: Hogarth Press, 1959.

———. "Inhibitions, Symptoms and Anxiety," 1926. Standard edition, vol. 20. London: Hogarth Press, 1959.

Fromm, Erich. *The Art of Loving.* New York: Bantam Books, 1956, p. 33.

Gaylin, Willard. *Caring.* New York: Alfred A. Knopf, 1976.

Gewirtz, J. L., ed. *Attachment and Dependency.* Washington, D.C.: V. H. Winston, 1972.

Goldfarb, W. "Psychological Privation in Infancy and Subsequent Adjustment." *American Journal of Orthopsychiatry* 15 (1945), pp. 247–55.

Harlow, H. F. and Zimmermann, R. R. "Affectional Responses in the Infant Monkey." *Science* 130 (1959), p. 421.

———. "Love in Infant Monkeys." *Scientific American* 200 (1959), pp. 68–74.

Huxley, Julian. *Man in the Modern World.* New York: Mentor Books, New American Library, 1944.

Kennell, John, Trause, Mary Anne, and Klaus, Marshall. *Evidence for a Sensitive Period in the Human Mother.* Ciba Books, forthcoming.

——. *Does Human Maternal Behavior after Delivery Show a Characteristic Pattern?* Ciba Books, forthcoming.

Klaus, M. D., Kennell, J. H., Plumb, N., and Zuehlke, S. "Maternal Behavior at the First Contact with Her Young," *Pediatrics* 46 (1970), pp. 187–92.

Maccoby, E. E., and Masters, J. C. "Attachment and Dependency." In P. H. Mussen (ed.), *Carmichael's Manual of Child Psychology.* 3rd ed. Vol. 2. New York: Wiley, 1970, pp. 73–158.

Mahler, M. S. "On Human Symbiosis and the Vicissitudes of Individuation." *Infantile Psychosis,* vol. 1. New York: International Universities Press, 1968.

Montagu, A. *Touching: The Human Significance of the Skin.* New York: Columbia University Press, 1971.

Piaget, J. *The Construction of Reality in the Child.* New York: Basic Books, 1954.

Portmann, Adolf. *Animals as Social Beings.* New York: Harper & Row, 1964.

Post, Seymour C. *Moral Values and the Superego Concept in Psychoanalysis.* New York: International Universities Press, 1972.

Rheingold, H., ed. *Maternal Behavior in Animals.* New York: Wiley, 1963.

Schaffer, H. R. "Some Issues for Research in the Study of Attachment Behavior." In Foss (ed.), *Determinants of Infant Behavior,* vol. 2. New York: Wiley, 1963, pp. 179–96.

Sears, R. "Attachment, Dependency and Frustration." In Gewirtz (ed.), *Attachment and Dependency, op. cit.,* pp. 1–27.

Spitz, R. A. "Hospitalization: An Inquiry into the Genesis of Psychiatric Conditions in Early Childhood," *The Psychoanalytic Study of the Child* 1 (1945), pp. 53–74.

——. *The First Year of Life.* New York: International Universities Press, 1965.

Tax, S. *Evolution After Darwin,* vol. 3, pp. 273–82, as quoted in Dobzhansky, *Mankind Evolving, op. cit.,* p. 22.

Winnicott, D. W. "The Theory of the Parent-Infant Relationship." *International Journal of Psychoanalysis* 41 (1960), pp. 585–95.

Yarrow, L. J. "Attachment and Dependency: A Developmental Perspective." In Gewirtz (ed.), *Attachment and Dependency, op. cit.,* pp. 81–95.

THEIR BROTHERS' KEEPERS:

AN EPISODE FROM ENGLISH HISTORY

Steven Marcus

DR. GAYLIN'S ARGUMENT IS IN GENERAL CONVINC-
ING, at least to me. I find no difficulty in accepting the
hypothesis that there is built into us some kind of
innate or genetic response of caring and loving and
that this response finds its clearest expression in the
ways we human beings deal with infants and small
children. Yet, accepting this hypothesis, and the biological or natural model it entails, compounds the difficulty of our problem. For something drastic seems to
occur, some virtually epistemological rupture seems
to take place, when we move from the biological to
the social, from the behavior of people as individuals
to their behavior in groups or as classes. It is almost as
if one might imagine two different kinds of human
beings within each of us: one who exists in the relatively "natural" life of the biological family, and another who exists in history; one who lives a personal
life and responds to others as persons, and one who
lives an institutional life and responds to others as
institutional functions. The difficulty we are faced
with is a difficulty of explanation. It is not, as Dr.
Gaylin argues, " 'merely' a technological problem." It
has to do with such imponderable questions as why
men in society and history behave as they do; why,
when they act in groups and as representatives of
certain kinds of classes, they often act as they never
would in other circumstances; why they seek to solve

certain problems by constructing certain kinds of institutions, and what it is that such institutions suggest to us about ourselves.

In what follows, such explanations are not achieved. I have tried to tell a story. Dr. Gaylin writes that the degree "to which we are nurtured and cared for during the days of our dependency will inevitably determine the degree to which we will be capable of nurturing and caring for others." The narrative account that I have drawn up is a sad one, and there is very little nurturing and caring for others in it; but there are no villains in it either. There is no evidence at all to suggest that any of the characters involved in the sorry circumstances I rehearse had anything but a happy infancy and childhood. And that too is part of our problem. How is it, we must continue to ask, that good people—decent, upright, and well-meaning citizens—can contrive, when they act on behalf of others and in the name of some higher principle or of some benign interest, to behave so harshly, coercively, and callously, so at odds with what they understand to be their good intentions. We may not be able to find satisfactory answers to such questions, but they are certainly worth pondering.

I should like to sketch briefly and with summary inadequacy a historical situation that seems to me exemplary of one part of the problem of dependency. At the beginning of the Industrial Age, with the extraordinary upheaval which that leap into modernism precipitated, a situation occurred which gave form to a good deal of subsequent thinking on dependency, as well as to some of the enduring difficulties and contradictions in the way in which the dependent are treated in modern society.

The situation I am referring to is what we have

generally come to call the problem of poverty—although it was not called by that name in late-eighteenth-century England, where the problem began to come to an acute head.* It developed not in London or the still undeveloped large towns, but on the land and in the countryside, where the traditional rural economy and organization of life were undergoing significant change. The customary provisions and obligations which supported and bound peasants to the land had, for the first time in Europe, disappeared. Land holdings were being consolidated on a very large scale. At the top were a small number of great landowners—noblemen or gentry; in the middle were the tenant farmers, who rented land from the great landowners and farmed it for profit; at the bottom was a rapidly increasing population of agricultural laborers, some of them former small tenant farmers, or cottagers, some extruded by recent enclosures of commons and waste lands, some former farm servants who had been let go as uneconomical propositions by their masters. In short, the typical English agricultural worker was a hired man, a rural proletarian, landless, and relying almost exclusively upon wage labor for his

*The following historical account makes no claims to originality. It is based entirely on the well-known and established primary and secondary sources and draws freely upon them. I have not hesitated to make wholesale use of many of the formulations arrived at in such sources. Among them are F. M. Eden, *The State of the Poor*, 3 vols., 1797; *Report of the Poor Law Commission*, 1834; S. and B. Webb, *History of English Local Government* I, VII–IX, 1906, 1927–29; J. L. Hammond and Barbara Hammond, *The Village Labourer*, 1760–1832, 1911; J. H. Clapham, *Economic History of Modern Britain*, I, 1926; Karl Polanyi, *The Great Transformation*, 1944; Samuel Finer, *The Life and Times of Edwin Chadwick*, 1952; David Roberts, *Victorian Origins of the Welfare State*, 1960; J. D. Chambers and G. E. Mingay, *The Agricultural Revolution*, 1966; W. E. Tate, *The English Village Community and the Enclosure Movements*, 1967; J. R. Poynter, *Pauperism and Society*, 1969; E. J. Hobsbawm and George Rude, *Captain Swing*, 1969.

support. Most of them, in other words, were former marginal cultivators who could not hold out—marginal cultivators being notoriously vulnerable, because they can rarely be self-sufficient over extended periods of time. (When it is said that they were rural proletarians, reference is being made to their economic position, not to their social condition or to their own consciousness of it.)

The organization of labor in England rested largely upon a series of late medieval laws based generally on the principles of regulation and paternalism. Under the Poor Laws of 1536 and 1601 and the Statute of Artificers of 1563, provisions were made for the enforcement of labor. This sounds odd or redundant until one recalls that in late medieval England almost everyone was thought "poor" who had to work, who did not command income sufficient to keep him in leisure, or who did not belong to the landed classes. Hence the term "poor" tended to coincide with the idea of "common people." (Merchants fell somewhere in the middle, and successful merchants customarily got out by buying land and entering the gentry.) It follows that the majority of freeborn Englishmen were also members of "the poor," and almost no one thought of the matter as a paradox, anymore than they felt it a paradox that the freeborn Englishman also had a right to support if he were temporarily unemployed. If he were unemployed he belonged for the time to the ranks of what were known as the able-bodied poor, later the deserving poor. In addition, the old, the chronically infirm or disabled, and orphaned children were all also freeborn Englishmen and had to be cared for in a society that declared that within its boundaries there was a place for every Christian soul. At the bottom of the heap were the paupers, those who for one reason or another declared themselves destitute of means of support and subsistence, and who, barren of substance, turned to their fellows for relief.

The Poor Law of 1601 declared that all the able-bodied poor must be put to work of some kind, so that they could be said to earn their sustenance; the sustenance itself was provided by the parish—the local unit of administration in England. The obligation of relief rested directly upon the parish itself, which therefore had to have the powers to raise the necessary funds by means of local taxes, called in England rates. These were levied on all householders and tenants in the parish, and the rates varied according to the value of the rental of either the land or the houses they inhabited.

Under the range of local regulations—there were nearly 16,000 Poor Law authorities in England—enormous differences in provisions for the poor would have to occur; and indeed they did, most of them tending in the direction of neglect and inadequacy. Still, up until the last third of the eighteenth century, the social fabric of village life remained largely intact. At that time, however, people began to be aware of a new, alarming, and mysterious phenomenon—rural pauperism began to rise and continued to rise. Something unprecedented was occurring; a *permanent* surplus of labor was coming into existence in the countryside. This was first a result of a population growth which started in about 1750; neither agricultural employment nor migration had risen in sufficient proportion to the population increase. At the same time the largest social upheaval in history since the neolithic revolution was about to break loose in England (and spread from there across the world), but no one at the time could possibly have known it. Indeed, there began to occur yet another unheard-of phenomenon: a boom in trade could coincide with increased unemployment, an increase in the distress of the poor, and a rise in relief. Poverty was now becoming very expensive. In such a situation, men behaved as they usually do—they began to fiddle with the administrative machinery to see if they could find ways to increase efficiency and reduce expenses, believing the machinery itself to be the proximate cause. In 1782, for example, Gilbert's Act went into effect. Under the provisions of this law the units of administration were to be expanded, and parish unions were to be set up at the behest of the parishes themselves. Parishes were urged to find work for the able-bodied poor in their neighborhoods; and in supplement to such work, outdoor relief and even occasional aid-in-wages, or cash supplements, were permitted in order to reduce the costs of relief to the able-bodied poor. In 1795, an immense fiddle was undertaken. This was a time of intense rural distress, virtual famine, and widespread unrest. So intense was it that the Act of Settlement (of 1662), which had placed restrictions on mobility and bound a laborer to his parish, was annulled, thereby setting the stage for the creation of a countrywide labor market. In May of that same year, moreover, the justices of the peace of the county of Berkshire decided to meet the great distress by a relatively new measure: subsidies in aid of wages were to be granted along a scale that depended on the price of bread. In effect, a minimum income of sorts was to be guaranteed to the poor, irrespective of their earnings. The resolution ran:

When the gallon loaf of second flour, weighing 8 lbs. 11 oz. shall cost 1 shilling, then every poor and industrious man shall have for his support 3 s. weekly, either produced by his own or his family's labor or an allowance from the poor rates, and for the support of his wife and every other of his family 1 s. 6 d. When the gallon loaf shall cost 1 s. 4 d., then every poor and industrious man shall have 4 s. for his own, and 1 s. 10 d. for the support of every other of his family. And so in proportion as the price of bread rises or falls (that is to say), 3 d. to the man and 1 d. to every other of the family, on every penny which the loaf rises above a shilling.

Introduced as an emergency measure, this system was in one form or another soon adopted throughout most of the countryside. At first it seemed that this piece of apparently liberal administrative change introduced the idea of a "right to live."* Actually, this paternalistic measure, which was in part intended to protect the agricultural and village working poor from the harsh effects of a new capitalist free market in labor, had a calamitous effect. Under the new system a working man got relief, even if he was working, as soon as his wages fell below the family subsistence income granted by the scale. With his meager income now guaranteed whatever his wages—and with the added certainty that he could never make more than that guaranteed subsistence—the laborer had little impetus to satisfy his employer. Conversely, the agricultural employer could now obtain labor at miniscule wages; whatever he paid, the subsidy from the poor rates brought the laborer's income up to the guaran-

---

*I think it is probably warranted for me to say that this account is not an allegory: that it is not intended to discredit notions of minimum incomes, or negative income taxes, or guaranteed wages of one or another kind. I am describing a specific historical set of circumstances, in a specific context, which had specific consequences. The inferences to be drawn from these circumstances are not allegorical ones.

teed minimum scale. It followed inevitably, we can now see, that within a few years the productivity of free labor dropped to that of pauper labor—thus providing another incentive for employers to keep wages low. There was no easy way out of this vicious circle.

And yet, as one historian of the period has ironically remarked, "No measure was ever more universally popular. Parents were free of the care of their children, and children were no longer dependent upon parents; employers could reduce wages at will, and workers were safe from hunger whether they were busy or slack; humanitarians applauded the measure as an act of mercy even though not of justice and the selfish gladly consoled themselves with the thought that though it was merciful at least it was not liberal."

A monster had been created. A long-term demoralization set in upon a countryside that was already demoralized. However long it took, the ordinary man was sooner or later pushed onto relief, and the countryside as a whole was moving toward pauperization and loss of self-respect. The freeborn Englishman's right to protection had been transformed into mass dependency, which, at the moment, seemed preferable to the rootless independence of a free wage laborer in an open market. And paradoxically, this preference led to the human degradation that is historically inseparable from the English experience of early capitalism in both town and country.

At the same time, however, ordinary people in the countryside tried to resist as best they could. They were precapitalistic in ethos and mentality, strongly touched by tradition, ruled in their behavior by motives that were not entirely economic. They did believe that they were freeborn Englishmen, and to them almost any kind of existence was preferable to that of a pauper. Nevertheless, they were becoming paupers outside of the poorhouse, on subsistence allowances. The squires and magistrates who thought up this device had hoped to restore stability to a countryside that they were themselves revolutionizing, while at the same time keeping wages down. In point of fact, they destabilized it in another direction and at an enormous human cost. At bottom they were trying to maintain the ancient ideal of a stable though unequal society, while combining it with those aspects of agrarian capitalism advantageous to landlords and farmers.

Summing things up, the historian E. J. Hobsbawm has remarked that agrarian capitalism of this period

> degenerated into a general lunacy, in which farmers were encouraged to pay as little as they could (since wages could be supplemented by the parish) and used the mass of pauper labor as an excuse for not raising their productivity; while their most rational calculation would be, how to get the maximum subsidy for their wage-bill from the rest of the rate-payers. Laborers, conversely, were encouraged to do as little work as they possibly could, since nothing could get them more than the official minimum of subsistence. If they worked at all, it was only because their fathers had done so before them, and because a man's self-respect required him to.

Thus degradation, dehumanization, and—economically—a fall in productivity went hand in hand. As poor rates rose along with falling productivity, the overseers of the Poor Law reacted predictably. The poor were starved even further. This became particularly clear toward the end of the Napoleonic wars, with the general fall in agricultural prices. Between 1815 and 1834 English poor law expenditure per unit of the population decreased by almost one-third and, as a percentage of the national income, by one-half. What this means, among other things, is that the subsistence minimum was itself progressively pared down—beginning from a base that in 1795 was hardly munificent. The coming of industrial society to the countryside brought immiseration that is difficult to describe. The English rural worker, who in the middle of the eighteenth century was the pride of his nation, had become fifty and one hundred years later broken, impoverished, and servile.

By making outdoor relief and supplementary wage payments general, the practice begun on a wide scale in 1795 dismantled the whole system of the traditional poor law. A universal system of pauperism had come into existence. Distinctions between workhouse and poorhouse disappeared. Working men upon the land, whether they were employed, unemployed, or paupers, now tended to become one anonymous and redundant mass of dependent poverty—all lining up in public each week to receive their miserable dole at the parish pay table. Everything was sinking into an indiscriminate morass of de-differentiated poverty. The system that appeared to be supporting them was in fact despoiling them. What seemed at first to be an extension of the traditional community supporting its less fortunate members among the lower orders turned out to be an extension of that part of the traditional community that exploited the lower orders and lived off their labor, although at the time no one was quite conscious of the circumstance in these terms.

The situation was so acute that from 1795 onward, in the midst of the wars that came out of the French Revolution, the best minds in the nation—along with some of the worst as well—occupied themselves with this subject. From 1796 to 1834 there took place the first concerted and extended discussion of the problem of poverty in the history of our culture. The schemes and proposals that were put forward varied from the hopeless to the horrible, and I cannot survey them here. I will only touch upon two of the major figures in this discussion. Malthus got into the picture very early on. His *Essay on the Principle of Population* was first published in 1798, and its gloomy view of human affairs helped deepen the dark atmosphere in which discussion took place. By 1803 Malthus had worked out a general position for himself on this matter. The only way to deal with the question of the dependent poor—the paupers—was to abolish the Poor Law altogether. Public relief does no good and must be withheld, he maintained, even from illegitimate and deserted children. Private charity was not condemned—it was after all a Christian act (and Malthus was a clergyman); but it was neither praised nor thought to be more than a minor palliative. If all relief were withheld, Malthus wrote, the poor would quickly learn "to defend themselves, [and] we might rest secure, that they would be fruitful enough in resources, and that the evils which were absolutely irremediable, they would bear with the fortitude of men, and the resignation of Christians." The dependent poor would have to learn moral restraint, and toward this end Malthus proposed to include sermons against marriage in the wedding service. As for the rest, he in effect suggested that "nature" should be reintroduced into society, that it should be allowed to take its course, and that, in sum, the dependent poor be abandoned. Mass death would come about in due course, and those who survived would have learned the virtues of self-dependence and self-sustainment. There

was a demented kind of logic in this: Malthus had his
followers, but the harshness of this proposal was too
much even for those harsh times.

It was not long before Jeremy Bentham began turning out papers on the question. Almost at once he saw
that his all-purpose building, the Panopticon, originally planned as a penitentiary, could do good service
as a workhouse (by which the convict and the pauper
became interchangeable). Bentham was against abolition, but he was for radical institutional reform, sys-
tematical and on a national scale. He proposed an
analytic division of the whole country; as an ideal, five
hundred great workhouses would be built, each 10 2/3
miles apart, so that no man would be more than half
a day's march from one. Economy of scale would thus
make for great savings. As for questions of settlement,
he proposed that all infants be branded, painlessly and
indelibly, with name, place, and date of birth; hence
identification for settlement and a score of other useful purposes would be easily ensured.

Like others at the time, Bentham was possessed
with the idea that the able-bodied poor and paupers
could be employed at a profit, and most of his mental
exertions were bent in that direction. The problem
was that the largest group of the pauperized were
children, or, as he put it, the "non-aged." He needed
to know their number and probable net value, so he
drew up his *Non-Adult Value Table,* and wrote to his
friends, asking what was the average child worth; was
it worth more or less than nothing? The answers that
he received have not been preserved. Bentham proposed that each huge workhouse be run as a business;
the salaries of governors would vary with both profit
and the rate of infant mortality in their houses. The
houses themselves would be run on the principles of

"Central Inspection" and "Separation and Aggregation" of the various classes of paupers. It was all planned in great detail, the point being that of maximum regulation over all inmates. Everyone was to work; even the blind were to knit. Child labor was the center of Bentham's employment plan. Indeed, he began to plan for "indigenous" paupers, who would be conceived, bred, and brought up in the house itself. Visions of a new society rose up off his manuscript paper.

The principle that governed this entire scheme and that fitted it into the actual society at large, however, was Bentham's masterstroke: the principle of less-eligibility. Although the Panopticon, to Bentham's bitter disappointment, was eventually rejected by a parliamentary committee in 1811 (Bentham received 23,000 pounds in compensation for his efforts), this principle was to have guided the great reform. According to it, if "the condition of persons maintained at the public charge were *in general* rendered *more eligible,* upon the whole, than that of persons maintained at their own charge, those of the latter number not excepted, whose condition is least eligible," then calamity would be inevitable. The only way things could work was to make the conditions of relief so odious, exigent, humiliating, and forbidding that one would do anything short of starving not to choose them. And when in 1834 the new Poor Law came into being, this was the rule that was essentially followed. The only thing worse than dependency would be death itself.

The law of 1834 was the most important piece of social legislation passed in the nineteenth century. It established a new model of administrative machinery —nationally centralized decision making on substantive issues of policy, professionalized civil servants, bureaucratic rationality. In essence it was the first recognizably modern welfare system. The new law provided that in future no outdoor relief be given; nor was there any aid-in-wages. The workhouse remained and that was it.* It was now up to the poor man to decide whether he was so bereft of the necessities of existence that he would volunteer to enter an institution that was deliberately designed as a place of horror and shame and stigma; where humiliation was openly forced upon him; where he was separated from his wife and children; where rigid rules of hygiene and cleanliness were made into excuses for further deprivations. The pauper's dependent incarceration now meant banishment from the community of the living. And if he died still a pauper, he was buried in a special pauper's graveyard—banished even in death from the community of the dead that the living preserve.

When the new law went into effect it was greeted with epic anger. No piece of legislation in English history has probably ever been so hated, execrated, and despised. The transformation, in many places, was abrupt and radical. The needy poor were left largely to their fate, and the "deserving poor" suffered bitterly, since they were in general too proud and upright to enter the workhouse, which had now become

---

*That was so in theory and to some degree, though not absolutely, in practice. It was simply impossible to impose complete uniformity of administration onto a complex and historically variegated society, and the administration of the new system varied from place to place. In many areas, the new system was installed; in others compromises with the old seemed to have been struck; and in others old practices were continued. In still others the new system had no bearing on the economic or social realities that prevailed therein. What mattered most, however, was the meaning of the new law, the intentions behind it, the social consensus among the ruling groups that it registered, and the manner in which it pointed toward the future and away from the past. In these senses it was a genuine social and cultural watershed.

a place of torture and torment. Thus it was that the English poor were compelled to be "independent" and were forced into the competitive labor market. Under the old system they had been taken care of rather like dependent, domestic animals; now they had to take care of themselves, and in the face of extremely difficult circumstances. In the old system there was the familiar misery of a deep-rooted degradation; in the new the working man was cast loose into a strange new world. He was free and independent in a new and unheard-of way. He was responsible for himself, and no one at this moment in the formation of a new society seemed responsible for him.

Two of England's greatest writers were on hand to comment on this monumental development. One wrote at the beginning of the process; one, some forty years later. William Wordsworth was a countryman, a native of Cumberland, and an inhabitant of the Lake District. He felt at home in the traditional rural community, saw that it was dying, and that certain forms of social life were going under. The independent statesmen of the dale, the shepherds and small crofters of his boyhood were perishing, and in poems like "The Last of the Flock" and "Michael" he described their passing away. Indeed Wordsworth felt that the older forms of social dependency within the community had something to be said for them. He even believed there was something to be said for beggars, and in one of his great early poems, "The Old Cumberland Beggar," he tries to say so. This beggar had been familiar to Wordsworth since he was a boy.

> Him from my childhood have I known; and then
> He was so old, he seems not older now;
> He travels on, a solitary man.

The beggar, alone, ancient, barely conscious, wanders on his endless round in the community. People know him and give him food, sometimes alms or coins. He is not useless, Wordsworth insists; he is not a nuisance. He is part of the habitual world of the community, and he even brings out feelings of kindliness and common obligation in all who see him regularly. He is a "silent monitor" to all who know him, and he is not to be pitied. For though he is dependent, there is also something independent about him as well. He is alone, but not in the way that the English poor would be alone some forty years later. Wordsworth moves his poem toward its conclusion with the following lines:

> Then let him pass, a blessing on his head!
> And, long as he can wander, let him breathe
> The freshness of the valleys; let his blood
> Struggle with frosty air and winter snows;
> And let the chartered wind that sweeps the heath
> Beat his grey locks against this withered face.
> Reverence the hope whose vital anxiousness
> Gives the last human interest to his heart.
> May never HOUSE, misnamed of INDUSTRY,
> Make him a captive!—for that pent-up din,
> Those life-consuming sounds that clog the air,
> Be his the natural silence of old age!
> Let him be free of mountain solitudes;
> And have around him, whether heard or not,
> The pleasant melody of woodland birds.
> Few are his pleasures: if his eyes have now
> Been doomed so long to settle upon earth
> That not without some effort they behold
> The countenance of the horizontal sun,
> Rising or setting, let the light at least
> Find a free entrance to their languid orbs.
> And let him, where and when he will, sit down
> Beneath the trees, or on a grassy bank
> Of highway side, and with the little birds

Share his chance-gathered meal; and, finally,
As in the eye of Nature he has lived,
So in the eye of Nature let him die!

In other poems Wordsworth chose similar solitary figures, figures who for him embodied the virtues of resolution and independence, as resonant of the qualities that he felt were central to his sense of the human, to his idea of humanity. These figures, always of poor people, often of old ones, were essential to his vision of what constituted human experience. They were at some extreme edge of existence, and yet they remained human. They are, and have long been acknowledged to be, among the most striking images of our humanity in English literature.

The second observer wrote some decades later and is the greatest of all English writers on dependency. I am referring of course to Dickens. There is hardly a form of dependency that he does not represent with inimitable power somewhere—including drug addiction; alcoholism; senility; madness; about every other form of infirmity, such as mental retardation and brain damage; hysterical paralysis; and poverty of almost every kind. His second novel, *Oliver Twist,* is a blistering satirical attack on the new Poor Law and on the principles that animated it, including the awareness that independence in the scheme of political economy was easily convertible into isolation and abandonment. He returned to this subject in his last completed novel, *Our Mutual Friend* (1864–65), and made there another representation of how the English poor regarded this law and the institution especially made for them. Some of the characters in this novel are seeking to adopt a child. They are told that they can find one in a town nearby. An old woman, Betty Higden, is caring for an infant. He is her great-grandson, the son of her granddaughter who has recently died. All her children and other grandchildren have died as well. She lives in a small cottage, takes in washing, and baby sits, getting four pence a week per child. Here are some passages about her:

> She was one of those old women, was Mrs. Betty Higden, who by dint of indomitable purpose and a strong constitution fight out many years, though each year has come with its new knock-down blows fresh to the fight against her, wearied by it; an active old woman, with a bright dark eye and a resolute face, yet quite a tender creature too; not a logically reasoning woman. . . .

She shows the visitors her grandchild, the children she is minding, and an odd youth, named Sloppy, who is her ward and who helps her with her various small chores. The visitors, led by a character called the Secretary, ask about him.

> "A love-child," returned Betty Higden, dropping her voice; "parents never known; found in the street. He was brought up in the—" with a shiver of repugnance, "—the House."
> "The Poor-House?" said the Secretary. Mrs. Higden set that resolute old face of hers, and darkly nodded yes.
> "You dislike the mention of it."
> "Dislike the mention?" answered the old woman. "Kill me sooner than take me there. Throw this pretty child under cart-horses' feet and a loaded waggon, sooner than take him there. Come to us and find us all a-dying, and set a light to us all where we lie, and let us all blaze away with the house into a heap of cinders, sooner than move a corpse of us there! . . .
> "Do I never read in the newspaper," said the dame,

fondling the child—"God help me and the like of me!
—how the worn-out people that do come down to
that, get driven from post to pillar, and pillar to post,
a purpose to tire them out! Do I never read how they
are put off, put off . . .—how they are grudged,
grudged, grudged the shelter, or the doctor, or the
drop of physic, or the bit of bread? Do I never read
how they grow heart sick of it and give it up, after
having let themselves drop so low, and how they after
all die out for want of help? Then I say, I hope I can
die as well as another, and I'll die without that disgrace. . . ."

"Johnny, my pretty," continued old Betty, caressing
the child, and rather mourning over it than speaking
to it, "your old Granny Betty is nigher fourscore year
than three-score and ten. She never begged nor had
a penny of the Union money in all her life. She paid
scot and she paid lot when she had money to pay; she
worked when she could, and she starved when she
must. You pray that your Granny may have strength
enough left her at the last . . . to get up from her bed
and run and hide herself, and sworn to death in a hole,
sooner than fall into the hands of those Cruel Jacks we
read of, that dodge and drive, and worry and weary,
and scorn and shame, the decent poor."

Betty does not want to part with her last surviving
descendant, but she is getting old, and has occasional
spells of weakness, and is afraid of leaving him alone
in the world.

"If I could have kept the dear child, without the
dread that's always upon me of his coming to that fate
I have spoken of, I could never have parted with him,
even to you. For I love him, I love him. . . . I love my
husband long dead and gone, in him; I love my children dead and gone, in him; I love my young and
hopeful days dead and gone, in him. I couldn't sell that
love, and look upon you in your bright kind face. It's

a free gift. I am in want of nothing. When my strength fails me, if I can but die out quick and quiet, I shall be quite content. I have stood between my dead and that shame I have spoken of, and it has been kept off from every one of them. Sewed into my gown," with her hand upon her breast, "is just enough to lay me in the grave. Only see that it's rightly spent, so as I may rest free to the last from that cruelty and disgrace, and you'll have done much more than a little thing for me, and all that in this present world my heart is set upon."

Later on in the novel, Betty begins seriously to sicken, and in order to further the chances of Sloppy, her ward, decides to run away. She asks for a loan of twenty shillings to fit herself out.

"There's a deadness steals over me at times. . . . Now, I seem to have Johnny in my arms—now, his mother —now his mother's mother—now, I seem to be a child again myself, a-lying once again in the arms of my own mother—then I get numbed, thought and senses, till I start out of my seat, afeerd that I'm a-growing like the poor old people that they brick up in the Unions, as you may some times see when they let'em out of the four walls to have a warm in the sun, crawling quite scared about the streets. I was a nimble girl, and have always been a active body. . . . I can still walk twenty mile if I am put to it. I'd far better be a-walking than a-getting numbed and dreary. I'm a good fair knitter, and can make many little things to sell. The loan from your lady and gentleman of twenty shillings to fit out a basket with would be a fortune for me. Trudging round the country and tiring of myself out, I shall keep the deadness off, and get my own bread by my own labour. And what more can I want?"

"And this is your plan," said the Secretary, "for running away?"

"Show me a better! My deary, show me a better! Why I know very well," said old Betty Higden, "and you know very well, that your lady and gentleman would set me up like a queen for the rest of my life, if so be that we could make it right among us to have it so. But we can't make it right among us to have it so. I've never took charity yet, nor yet has any one belonging to me. And it would be forsaking of myself indeed, and forsaking of my children dead and gone, and forsaking of their children dead and gone, to set up a contradiction now at last."

"It might come to be justifiable and unavoidable at last," the Secretary gently hinted, with a slight stress on the word.

"I hope it never will! It ain't that I mean to give offence by being anyways proud," said the old creature simply, "but that I want to be of a piece like, and helpful of myself right through to my death."

So Betty goes off, and later still we see her on her pilgrimage, moving toward her end.

Old Betty Higden fared upon her pilgrimage as many ruggedly honest creatures, women and men, fare on their toiling way along the roads of life. Patiently to earn a spare bare living, and quietly to die, untouched by work-house hands—that was her highest sublunary hope. . . .

The poor old creature had taken the upward course of the river Thames as her general track. . . . She would take her stand in market-places, where there were such things, on market-days; at other times, in the busiest . . . portion of the little quiet High Street; at still other times she would explore the outlying roads for great houses, and would ask leave at the Lodge to pass in with her basket, and would not often get it. But ladies in carriages would frequently make purchases from her trifling stock, and were usually pleased with her bright eyes and her hopeful speech. In these and her clean dress originated a fable that she was well to do: one might say, for her station, rich. As making a comfortable provision for its subject which costs nobody anything, this class of fable has long been popular. . . .

But the old abhorrence grew stronger on her as she grew weaker, and it found more sustaining food than she did in her wanderings. Now, she would light upon the shameful spectacle of some desolate creature—or some wretched ragged groups of either sex, or of both sexes, with children among them, huddled together like the smaller vermin, for a little warmth—lingering and lingering on a doorstep, while the appointed evader of the public trust did his dirty office of trying to weary them out and so get rid of them. Now, she would light upon some poor decent person, like herself, going afoot on a pilgrimage of many weary miles to see some worn-out relative or friend who had been charitably clutched off to a great blank barren Union House, as far from old home as the County Jail (the remoteness of which is always its worst punishment for small rural offenders), and in its dietary, and in its lodging, and in its tending of the sick, a much more penal establishment. Sometimes she would hear a newspaper read out, and would learn how the Registrar General cast up the units that had within the last week died of want and of exposure to the weather: for which that Recording Angel seemed to have a regular fixed place in his sum, as if they were its halfpence. All such things she would hear discussed . . . and from all such things she would fly with the wings of raging Despair.

This is not to be received as a figure of speech. Old Betty Higden, however tired, however footsore, would start up and be driven away by her awakened horror of falling into the hands of charity. It is a remarkable Christian improvement, to have made a pursuing Fury of the Good Samaritan; but it was so in this case, and it is a type of many. . . .

The end is now rapidly drawing near.

The morning found her afoot again, but fast declining as to the clearness of her thoughts, though not as to the steadiness of her purpose. Comprehending that her strength was quitting her, and that the struggle of her life was almost ended, she could neither reason out the means of getting back to her protectors, nor even form the idea. The overmastering dread, and the proud stubborn resolution it engendered in her to die undegraded, were the two distinct impressions left in her failing mind. Supported only by a sense that she was bent on conquering in her life-long fight, she went on.

The time was come, now, when the wants of this little life were passing away from her. She could not have swallowed food, though a table had been spread for her in the next field. The day was cold and wet, but she scarcely knew it. She crept on, poor soul, like a criminal afraid of being taken, and felt little beyond the terror of falling down while it was yet daylight, and being found alive. She had no fear that she would live through another night.

Sewn in the breast of her gown, the money to pay for her burial was still intact. If she could wear through the day, and then lie down to die under cover of the darkness, she would die independent. If she were captured previously, the money would be taken from her as a pauper who had no right to it, and she would be carried to the accursed work house. Gaining her end, the letter would be found in her breast, along with the money, and the gentle folks would say when it was given back to them, "She prized it, did old Betty Higden, she was true to it; and while she lived, she would never let it be disgraced by falling into the hands of those that she held in horror." Most illogical, inconsequential, and light-headed, this; but travellers in the valley of the shadow of death are apt to be light-headed; and worn-out people of low estate have a trick of reasoning as indifferently as they live, and doubtless would appreciate our Poor Law more philosophically on an income of ten thousand a year.

So, keeping to by-ways, and shunning human approach, this troublesome old woman hid herself, and fared on all through the dreary day. Yet so unlike was she to vagrant hiders in general, that sometimes, as the day advanced, there was a bright fire in her eyes, and a quicker beating at her feeble heart, as though she said exultingly, "The Lord will see me through it!" . . . Faring on and hiding, hiding and faring on, the poor harmless creature, as though she were a Murderess and the whole country were up after her, wore out the day and gained the night.

Finally she reaches her last goal and resting place, a tree among a grove of trees.

She placed her orderly little basket at her side, and sank upon the ground, supporting herself against the tree. It brought to her mind the foot of the Cross, and she committed herself to Him who died upon it. Her strength held out to enable her to arrange the letter in her breast, so that it could be seen that she had a paper there. It had held out for this, and it departed when she had done.

There follows the scene of her death, which is as deeply moving as what has led up to it.

This is what men in the past made of one another, and this is one way as well in which people contrived to survive the vicissitudes in which poverty, misfortune, and their fellows' own efforts to help had placed them. The hell that the English poor went through cannot be redeemed by a few great writers who were their friends and sympathizers. That they went through it at all and came out alive is testimony in itself to a kind of human strength we can all admire.

Yet I do not want to leave this topic without suggesting that things might have been much worse. Indeed, only a decade after the new Poor Law came into operation, the English themselves demonstrated how much worse things might have been. I am referring to the Irish famine and the behavior of the English governing classes during that historical disaster. This is not the place to discuss the matter in any detail,* but what the English did was, in effect, to abandon an entire nation that existed in circumstances of extreme and complicated dependency. Ireland was left, as one high official suggested, to the "operation of natural causes." And another influential figure of the time, Nassau Senior, political economist and advisor on economic affairs to the British government, remarked that he "feared that the famine of 1848 in Ireland would not kill more than a million people, and that would scarcely be enough to do much good." Neither of the men who made these statements—and they are representative remarks—was a bad or cruel person, anymore than the Poor Law reformers were bad or cruel as individual persons; and I do not think that one can argue that the abandonment of the Irish was not more drastic, regressive, and inhumane than the coercive treatment of the English poor. The English treatment of the Irish was monstrous; it is historically unforgivable. By comparison—if comparisons in such a context mean very much—the English treatment of their own poor, brutal and harsh as it was, had here and there some glimmerings of sense and hope and held out some possibility of amelioration. Yet the point to be taken, I think, is that in both these historical situations of dependency men of good will were led to behave as they did by good intentions and reasonable sensibilities. There is a lesson to be learned here.

So I imagine what I am saying—and I imagine what I have learned—is that we can degrade people by

*I have done so in "Hunger and Ideology," *Representations* (New York, 1976), pp. 3–16.

caring for them; and we can degrade them by not caring for them; and in matters such as these there are neither simple answers nor simple solutions. We have gotten to this complex place, and we are not going to get away from it in a hurry. We belong to a reformist tradition, and long experience should have made us skeptical by now of some of our best-intentioned efforts. Caring for people in a concerted effort and not caring for them in a concerted effort are each of them, as matters of policy, interventions. All interventions have consequences, and one of the things we should learn to keep in the forefront of our consciousness is that the most important consequences of any intervention almost always turn out to be those consequences that were not intended or planned upon or could not have been calculated beforehand. Dependents, precisely because they are dependent and often unable to help themselves, deserve more than others to be protected from the unintended consequences of our benevolence and the incalculable consequences of our social good will.

THE STATE
AS PARENT:

SOCIAL POLICY IN
THE PROGRESSIVE
ERA

David J. Rothman

In the history of American attitudes and practices toward the dependent, no group more energetically or consistently attempted to translate the biological model of the caring parent into a program for social action than the Progressives. The Progressive tradition that took hold in the United States during the first two decades of the twentieth century and persisted right through the middle of the 1960s gave a remarkable primacy to the idea of the state as parent. Far more than a rhetorical flourish or convenient metaphor with which to galvanize public support, this concept shaped reformers' definitions of the proper realm for state action and, perhaps even more important, the appropriate methods for the state to adopt in fulfilling its goals. The ideal dictated not only the ends but the means of doing good.

As one would expect from such an orientation, Progressives were far more attentive to the "needs" of disadvantaged groups than to their "rights." Needs were real and obvious—the poor were overworked and underpaid, living in unhealthy tenements and working in miserable sweatshops. Rights, on the other hand, were "so-called"—the right of the poor to sleep under the bridge or the right of the laborer to fix his own contract with an all-powerful corporation. Clearly, a reform platform that looked to needs expanded the boundaries of political intervention, legitimating a wide range of ameliorative action; the state as parent had a lengthy agenda to accomplish. But the concept cut two ways: those in need of help were more or less like children. The disadvantaged were the objects of care, they were to be done for. They did not require protection against the well-meaning parent, rights to be exercised against the paternalistic state.

It is not claiming too much to assert that this perspective was at the core of liberalism in modern America, uniting, for all their minor differences, the first settlement-house workers with later New and Fair Dealers. One can identify a mainstream reform position in the period 1900–1965 that shared a basic agreement on the principles that should guide a benevolent social policy. To be sure, there were critics to either side, socialists and Marxists to the left who defined Progressives as no more than tinkerers with a fundamentally corrupt capitalist organization, and conservatives to the right who saw their interventions as destructive of the essential integrity of the system. Nevertheless, the Progressives enjoyed a centrality and an influence that marked them off in a special way and that enables us to talk meaningfully, if in shorthand terms, of *the reformers.* Then, rather suddenly, beginning in the mid-1960s and continuing to our day, this tradition came under a novel, vigorous, and even bitter attack emanating not from the far left or far right, but—and in more than a metaphorical sense— from the children of Progressivism. We are now, in ways and for reasons that this essay will explore, in a post-Progressive period. A new generation of reformers, drawn to an unprecedented degree from the ranks of lawyers and the dependent groups themselves, are pitting rights against needs, or, to put it more broadly, are challenging the wisdom and propriety of an ideal of the state as parent and the dependent as child. They are highly critical of Progressivism not merely for pragmatic reasons—for what it did or did not manage to accomplish—but for conceptual reasons: for importing a misguided and ultimately mischievous model into the political arena.

Given the centrality of Progressive thinking in this country, it is appropriate to place the contemporary objections to this tradition in still another light. An arrow that the late critic Lionel Trilling once aimed at the far left would now seem to many observers an appropriate barb to hurl against liberalism itself. In 1947 Trilling published an essay, "Manners, Morals and the Novel," in which he elegantly set out his case against Marxist reform. (Indeed, in his novel of the same period, *The Middle of the Journey,* Trilling had Gilbert Maxim, his disillusioned ex-Communist character, voice a variant on this same argument.) Trilling defended the novel for its ability to strip away illusions, to go beyond hyperbolic rhetoric so as to uncover the hidden realities. His praise for such novelists as Balzac, James, and Forster—indeed for the whole genre—reflected a commitment to what he called "moral realism." Moral realism, he explained, taught us "that to act against social injustice is right and noble but that to choose to act so does not settle all moral problems but on the contrary generates new ones of an especially difficult sort." We have so many books, Trilling commented, "that praise us for taking progressive attitudes." We sorely lack those that "ask what might lie behind our good impulses." He fully appreciated that "anything that complicates our moral fervor in dealing with reality . . . must be regarded with some impatience." Yet it was just this impatience that worried him and must worry us. "Moral passions are even more willful and imperious and impatient than the self-seeking passions. All history is at one in telling us that their tendency is to be not only liberating but restrictive." And so he concluded in a sentence that has taken on a new relevance: "Some paradox in our nature leads us, once we have made our fellow men the objects of our enlightened interest, to go on to make them the objects of our pity, then of our wisdom, ultimately of our coercion."

This phrase brings us to the very heart of the current dissatisfactions with Progressivism, for to its critics the movement suffered deeply from an absence of moral realism. Its proponents were so attached to a paternalistic model that they never concerned themselves with the potential of their programs to be as coercive as they were liberating. In their eagerness to play parent to the child, they did not pause to ask whether the dependent had to be protected against their own well-meaning interventions. It was as if the benevolence of their motives together with their clear recognition of the wretchedness of lower-class social conditions guaranteed that ameliorative efforts would unambiguously benefit the poor. The problem, it now appears, is not only that Progressives could not accomplish their grand designs but that policies whose legitimacy rested on their promise to do good may actually have produced substantial harms.

Each generation has its own favorite brand of horror stories, its own special set of circumstances that prick its conscience and goad it to action. For Progressives, it was instances of neglect; the state had to intervene to correct inequities. The Jacob Riis and Lewis Hine photographs revealed little waifs selling newspapers on street corners or tending oversized mill looms.

The tracts of Jane Addams and Lillian Wald pointed to the desperate need of widows left to their own devices, the horrors of families broken up with the mother entering an almshouse and her children an orphan asylum. Surely men and women of good will ought to be able to halt such practices, and public resources had to be devoted to improving their living conditions. To choose to act against such gross social injustice had to be right and noble, and anything that complicated one's response to these wretched circumstances seemingly had to be treated with impatience.

Now a new kind of horror story has gained popularity. It is aptly represented in the case of Mrs. Lake, a Washington "bag lady," who carried her worldly possessions in two shopping bags. Mrs. Lake went out one day to the Department of Justice to press a claim for a pension; her efforts were unsuccessful, and as she left the Justice building, a police officer, a woman police officer at that, spotted her as someone who might be in need of assistance. Mrs. Lake appeared disoriented in the downtown district. The policewoman asked her for her home address, which Mrs. Lake was unable to supply; and although she had found her way to the Justice Department, the officer believed she could not find her way back home again. In short order, Mrs. Lake was confined to St. Elizabeth's Mental Hospital for "wandering," in mind and body, and despite her persistent efforts to be released from the institution, she remained there, for the rest of her days, ostensibly for her own good. Betty Higden won her battle; Mrs. Lake lost.

That Mrs. Lake's misfortune typifies the prevailing horror stories is another indication of the nature of the attack now being mounted against Progressivism. Put most succinctly, the commitment to paternalistic state intervention in the name of equality is giving way to a commitment to restrict intervention in the name of liberty. If our predecessors were determined to test the maximum limits for the exercise of state power in order to correct imbalances, we are about to test the minimum limits for the exercise of state power in order to enhance autonomy. The dialogue between these two approaches now dominates social policy discussions on dependency, and a close analysis of the assumptions and records of each position may well clarify, and perhaps even advance, the debates.

The Progressives' allegiance to a model of the state as parent rested on a series of propositions all of which seemed to confirm the validity and desirability of their approach. For one, Progressives were convinced that the sum of individual self-interested actions could no longer be counted upon to produce the common good. The nineteenth-century assumption of such a coincidence disappeared with the rise of the cities, business trusts, and immigrant ghettos. As Herbert Croly brilliantly argued, "No preestablished harmony can then exist between the free and abundant satisfactions of private needs and the accomplishment of a morally and socially desirable result." Rather, he insisted, "the American problem is a social problem"; the nation stood in need of "a more highly socialized democracy." To realize the promise of American life, the public sector would have to dominate the private sector. The state, not the individual, would define the common good and see to its fulfillment. In short, the major tenet of Progressive thought was that only the state could make the individual free. Only the enlarged authority of the government could satisfy the particular needs of all the citizens.

Further, Progressives had little doubt of the state's

ability to fulfill this charge or, put another way, of the ability of their programs to accomplish their goals. For one, their ranks were composed of the graduates of the new universities, those who had typically spent most of their classroom hours learning the canons of social science. They had been taught to investigate social reality with a clear eye to its improvement. The facts of the case—whether the rates of tuberculosis in the slums or the number of families poverty-stricken because of industrial accidents—would not only locate the source of the problem but at once compel ameliorative action. Progressive tracts and testimony at hearings were filled with statistical tables—as if the data would insure the success of their legislative efforts.

Progressives, in ways that cannot help but make contemporary analysts nostalgic, also shared a remarkable consensus on the goals for reform. There was no crisis of values that had to be debated, no agonizing consideration of the comparative worth of different life-styles. To Progressives, all Americans were to enter the ranks of the middle class. The melting-pot metaphor implied not only an amalgam of immigrants into a common mold, but an amalgam of classes into a common mold. Everyone was to respect private property, send their children to school, and give up whatever vices—particularly intemperance—that they might have brought with them from the old world, in order to become hardworking and law-abiding. "It is fatal for a democracy to permit the formation of fixed classes," argued that leading Progressive reformer, John Dewey; and one Progressive institution after another, from schools to settlement houses, set out to bridge the gap between the upper classes and the lower classes, between native-born and immigrants. The traffic across this bridge, of course, was to move only in one way, from them to us, from alien to American, from lower class to middle class.

This certain sense of direction among Progressives testified finally, and most significantly, to their keen sense of the essential viability—indeed superiority—of the American system. They stood ready to make immigrants over in their own image because ultimately they did not doubt that this course was in everyone's best interest. No sense of conflict of interests among classes or even among different groups within the same class complicated their analysis. Yes, some greedy businessmen would have to give up excess profits; some greedy speculators would have to be curbed. But no one's "true" or "real" interests (at least as reformers defined them) would be violated. The economic pie was infinitely expandable. The poor need not rise up against the rich to obtain their fair share. Social mobility promised that all of the deserving would climb the ladder, no one had to remain stuck at the bottom. Thus, that which promoted the stability of the society promoted the welfare of its members. Social cohesion and individual betterment went hand in hand.

Armed with these principles, Progressives enacted a series of novel measures designed to prevent and to relieve dependency and deviancy. Between 1900 and 1920 practically every state passed widow-pension laws, what we know today as Aid to Dependent Children. Heretofore, unless rescued by a private charitable society, the mother and her children had entered institutions; now public funds were to be expended to keep the family together at home. At the same time, practically every major city organized juvenile courts to handle cases of dependency and delinquency. In informal hearings, these special courts would decide, at their own discretion, what was in the best interests of the neglected or delinquent child. Moreover, juvenile courts as well as adult criminal courts began to organize and administer probation departments. Instead of sending youthful or minor offenders to an institution, the court could now sentence them to probation, leaving them in the community under the supervision of an officer.

It is clear that the Progressives were the first American reformers to perceive and to be outraged by the miseries that were endemic to the modern industrial system. The wretchedness of the almshouses—let alone the cruelty of separating the widow from her children, and the injuries inflicted by locking ten-year-olds in a stinking and filthy jail—were terribly real. No one is belittling the good conscience of the Progressives or their effort to go beyond a simple moralism that blamed the poor for their poverty. But what is at issue is how they moved to correct these evils. It is not so much their definitions of what constituted a social problem as the assumptions with which they attempted to ameliorate it that are now controversial.

The design of each of the Progressives' programs assumed a nonadversarial relationship between the state and the client. Since the state, whether in the guise of the juvenile court judge or probation officer or welfare administrator, was to help and not to punish the poor or the criminal, it was unnecessary—in fact it was counterproductive—to limit or to circumscribe officials' discretionary powers. Indeed, since no conflicts of interest divided the welfare of society from that of the dependent or deviant, Progressives were still more determined to endow the state with all necessary authority to fulfill its goals. The great discovery of the juvenile court, noted one reformer, was that "individual welfare coincided with the well-being of the state. Humanitarian and social considerations thus recommended one and the same procedure. . . . Sympathy, justice and even the self-interest of society were all factors in bringing about the changed attitude." The state could do good without sacrificing anyone's interests, without having to make trade-offs.

In each instance, therefore, enabling legislation and agency practice enhanced the prerogatives of state officials and reduced—and almost eliminated—legal protections and rights for those coming under their authority. To call the acts "widow pensions" was really a misnomer. The widows did not receive their allowance as a matter of right, the way a pensioner received his. Rather, the widow had to apply for her stipend, demonstrate her qualifications, her economic need, and her moral worth, and then trust to the decision of the welfare board. At their pleasure, and by their reckoning, she then obtained or did not obtain help. By the same token the juvenile court proceedings gave no standing to the whole panoply of rights that offenders typically enjoyed, from a trial by jury to assistance from counsel, to protections against self-incrimination. There was nothing atypical about the juvenile court judge who openly admitted that in his Minnesota courtroom "the laws of evidence are sometimes forgotten or overlooked." So too, probation officers were not bound by any of the restrictions that might fetter the work of police officers. They did not need a search warrant to enter a probationer's home, for as another juvenile court judge explained: "With the great right arm and force of the law, the probation officer can go into the home and demand to know the cause of the dependency or the delinquency of a child.

. . . He becomes practically a member of the family and teaches them lessons of cleanliness and decency, of truth and integrity." So caught up were reformers with this image of officer as family member that they gave no heed to the coercive character of their programs. To the contrary, they frankly declared that "threats may be necessary in some instances to enforce the learning of the lessons that he teaches, but whether by threats or cajolery, by appealing to their fear of the law or by rousing the ambition that lies latent in each human soul, he teaches the lesson and transforms the entire family into individuals which the state need never again hesitate to own as citizens." With the state eager and able to accomplish so beneficent a goal, there appeared no reason to restrict its actions.

The prevalence of such judgments among Progressives practically blinded them to the realities that followed on the enactment of their proposals. Not only did they fail to see the many inadequacies that quickly emerged in day-to-day operations, worse yet, they could not begin to understand that the programs might be administered in the best interests of officials, not clients. In the case of widow pensions, state legislatures appropriated niggardly amounts of funds for relief, so that only a handful of needy cases were served, and the monies that even they received were too limited to allow them to subsist. In effect, the widow had to open her life to the investigatory impulses of her social worker and at the same time still find work to supplement her dole. And those ineligible for even these paltry funds had to bear both the stigma of being labeled unworthy while they too desperately tried to make ends meet. The widow-pension program may have soothed the conscience of reformers—the state was now committed to the care of the worthy widow and her children—but it certainly did not solve the problem that they had originally addressed.

The operation of the juvenile court was no more satisfactory. Judges had unbounded discretion to do as they saw fit, and there was little recourse from their decisions. They still relied upon state reformatories and training schools to discipline the young, only now they justified their sentences, and not cynically either, in the language of rehabilitating the offender instead of punishing him. To incarcerate the young, a Pennsylvania court ruled in upholding the constitutionality of juvenile court sentences, was not to deprive them of their liberty. Commitments to reformatories under the new laws do not contemplate "restraint upon the natural liberty of children." The state was merely assuming the privileges that parents enjoy, exercising the "wholesome restraint which a parent exercises over his child. . . . No constitutional right is violated but one of the most important duties which organized society owes to its helpless members is performed." And the administration of probation was still less successful. Reformers had looked to a group of well-trained officers counseling a small number of clients. In fact, the probation officers were poorly trained, ill-equipped to do very much good at all, and, in any event, there was little that the best-intentioned of them could accomplish when carrying case loads of two to three hundred.

It may well also be that probation, which presented itself as an alternative to incarceration, served more frequently as a supplement to incarceration. The same numbers still went to institutions; the difference was that cases which had once been dismissed or suspended now came under the supervisory network of probation officers. To be sure, the encroachments on the civil liberties of many but certainly not all of the clients were generally not egregious because of the incredible case loads that probation officers carried. But that simply meant that the coerciveness of the state was limited only by the unwillingness of legislators to spend taxpayer money. It is an odd but perhaps accurate conclusion to note that the dependent and deviant may owe what freedom they have more to the fiscal conservatism of elected officials than to the benevolent motives of reformers.

Finally, Progressives' sense of paternalism enabled them to move in harsh and stringent ways against those that they believed to be irreformable and beyond rehabilitation—namely, the recidivist, the defective, the mentally retarded, and the unworthy poor. Since they had designed programs that would keep reformable types out of institutions and in the community, those that they defined as beyond help deserved incarceration, and incarceration for very long periods of time. Accordingly, many Progressives accepted the eugenic arguments of the time and were eager to confine the retarded for life, particularly the borderline retarded who might pass as normals and so go on to propagate a race of defectives. Some Progressives were also ready to sterilize the retarded, to make that operation the prerequisite for release into the community. And in a similar spirit, almost all Progressives were prepared to define broadly the category of PINS, persons in need of supervision, so that the state could move quickly to remove children from parents deemed unworthy, those children, in the language of one reformer, who had been raised in homes "in which they had been accustomed from their earliest infancy to drunkenness, immorality, obscene and vulgar language, filthy and degraded conditions of living."

This sketch of the Progressive tradition has a dual relevance to our understanding of contemporary American attitudes and policies toward the dependent. First, and most obviously, we are today well aware of the record of failure of these programs. We recognize that widow pensions did not reduce or eliminate poverty, that the juvenile court did not eradicate delinquency, that probation was hardly a panacea for crime. But such knowledge is really of minor import. Merely because programs did not work in the past does not mean that they might not work in the future. In no simple sense does history repeat itself. Perhaps less stingy legislatures, perhaps a more munificent federal government, would fund these programs fully and we would then witness their achievements.

Far more important, therefore, to the contemporary sense of dependency is the fact that the underlying assumptions of the Progressive stance no longer seem valid. What is remarkable about current reformist thinking is how far it has moved from these premises, how fundamentally it has rejected every major point in the synthesis.

To characterize this transformation in summary fashion there now exists a widespread and acute suspicion of the very notion of doing good among widely divergent groups on all points of the political spectrum. To claim to act for the purposes of benevolence was once sufficient to legitimate a program; at this moment it is certain to create suspicion. To announce that you are prepared to intervene for the best interests of some other person or party is guaranteed to provoke the quick, even knee-jerk, response that you are masking your true, self-interested, motives.

Whereas once historians and policy analysts were prone to label some movements reforms, thereby assuming their humanitarian aspects, they are presently far more comfortable with a designation of social control, thereby assuming their coercive quality. Not that one or the other approach is necessarily more intellectually fruitful. Rather, fashions have changed. The prevailing perspective looks first to how a measure may regulate the poor, not relieve them.

So too, we share a very acute sense of the failure of institutions to fulfill their caretaker responsibilities. Whereas Progressive reformers did recognize, indeed, by the recurring nature of scandals were compelled to recognize, the inadequacy of institutions— whether reformatories, orphan asylums, or almshouses—invariably they blamed the frugality of legislators, or the incompetence of administrators, or the cupidity of superintendents for the failures. The system was benign; the problem was with its implementation. Now, to the contrary, the system, the very idea of incarceration for the purposes of rehabilitation, is suspect among a surprisingly diverse group of observers, from federal judges to members of state investigatory commissions on nursing homes and juvenile corrections. And not only do a host of more or less well-designed research projects unanimously report on the failure of institutions to be rehabilitative, but a strong and compelling theoretical analysis, such as offered by Erving Goffman in *Asylums*, insists that incarceration by its very nature will inevitably infantilize the inmate and make his future adaptation to society more problematic.

This suspicion of benevolence and antiinstitutionalism has encouraged and is reinforced by an acute distrust of discretionary authority. It no longer seems appropriate to endow public or private officials with a wide latitude for the exercise of their authority. Since neither their motives, which are assumed to be social control, nor their decisions, which might well involve commitment to an institution, now seem acceptable, their prerogatives and powers must be carefully defined, bound in and circumscribed through detailed and precise laws and regulations. The formula is clear: better that a few should suffer from the inflexibility of a code than that the many should suffer through the discretion of an administrator.

Of the fact of this reversal there can be no question. We are in full revolt against the Progressive synthesis. But the more complicated and intriguing question, the answers to which must be more suggestive than definitive, is why this change should have occurred. Why is it that reformers in the 1970s are far more receptive to Trilling's call for moral realism? Why are they so much more comfortable with labels like "social control" and titles like "Regulating the Poor"? Why are they more prepared to rely upon procedural protections than purity of motive? Why is it that while they may grant the accuracy of a biological or psychoanalytic finding of the significance of altruism in many species, they are terribly reluctant to allow such a conclusion to structure social policy? Or, finally, why are they leaving an equality model to test the limits of a liberty model?

To begin to formulate an answer to these questions (or at least to recast them in a still broader context), it is appropriate to note first that these developments are part of a pervasive distrust of all constituted authorities, a general decline in the legitimacy of the authority of a whole series of persons and institutions. The list of those who have suffered this loss is as lengthy as it is revealing: college presidents and deans, high school principals and teachers, husbands and parents, psychiatrists, doctors, research scientists, and, obviously, prison wardens, social workers, hospital superintendents, and mental hospital superintendents. Many of us, either as objects of power or as wielders of power, have experienced this diminution quite directly. To choose but one example, many of us can remember from our own college days the phenomenon of dean's discipline. Having broken some rule or other, a rule which we had probably learned of through an informal student network, we shuffled into the dean's office, sheepishly, head hanging. We told our story, bringing up every exculpatory fact we could imagine, and then sat back hoping for the best. The dean pronounced the punishment, and, mumbling our apologies, we more or less backed out of the office. Such times are over. The student appears not before a dean in the privacy of his office but before a tribunal, whose composition reflects the working of a mathematical formula that brings so many administrators together with so many professors and so many students from the several university divisions. If the charge is of any significance, the student comes with his lawyer. Examination and cross-examination goes on: did the student have a printed, formally distributed listing of the college rules? Was his identity in the incident established beyond a reasonable doubt? And once the hearing is over, the tribunal retires, like a jury, to make its deliberations and reach its verdict. If the student is unhappy with the finding, he will move the case immediately into the courts, where the attention to procedural protections will be only somewhat more rigorous than what was practiced at the original hearing.

So too, the freewheeling exercise of disciplinary authority by high school officials is under challenge. Hearings and legal representation may well become the rule here. And more and more patients are refusing to sign the blanket release form that gives a doctor and his hospital the right to do whatever they think "necessary" to the person's body. Some research scientists are even discovering that their research protocols have to be carefully negotiated not just with the university and government committees on experimentation, but with the community at large. And if the community does not like what is afoot, as was the case, for example, with research into minimal brain dysfunction in Boston's schools, they will exercise political power, often successfully, to terminate the work. Marriage contracts that once vaguely spelled out duties of loving, cherishing, and, yes, obeying, may give way to contracts that detail who will carry out household duties on alternate days. And whereas once it was assumed that parents would invariably act in the best interests of the child, even in the midst of divorce proceedings, now it seems the better part of wisdom to have children represented by their own attorney. Indeed, before parents can commit their child to a mental hospital, it is becoming obligatory that the child be represented separately by an attorney.

In effect, reform policy presupposes a conflict of interests among these parties, conflicts which before were never admitted to or acknowledged. The assumption is that deans will act for the best interest of the university, not the student; that husbands will further their own needs, not their wives'; that parents will satisfy their own desires, not necessarily their children's; that research scientists have their own agenda of priorities that need not fit with the welfare of their subjects; that wardens' first thought is to the prison and not the inmate; and that psychiatrists will be more concerned with the health of the hospital than with the health of the patient. The Progressives' assumption that interests coincided, that the welfare of all parties could be satisfied, has become a thing of the past. Now the game seems to be a zero-sum game: if one party wins, another loses; if you are not one up, you are one down.

To put these changes into still another framework, we are witnessing the dissolution of the Progressive version of community as a viable concept, indeed the breakdown of normality as a viable concept. To many critics, there no longer seems to be a common weal that can be defined or appealed to as a justification for action. The very notion of a harmony of interests seems deceptive and mischievous. Not only can no one agree on what is good for all of us, no one can agree on what is proper behavior for any one of us. No consensus allows for a clear and uncontroversial division between sane and insane behavior, no unity exists around the once self-evident proposition that it is better to be sane rather than insane. As to any effort to define what constitutes normal sexual behavior—one has only to raise this point to recognize immediately how absurd any such attempt would be.

There is far more agreement on the reality of this state of affairs than on its merits. Some observers describe these developments in terms of loss and corruption, searching, logically enough, for a way to restore a sense of community, to revive the social contract, or, in Daniel Bell's formulation, to rebuild a sense of civitas among citizens. Somehow or other, through the family, or the church, or a new ideology, we will recreate bonds of trust, commonality of goals, a system in which all institutions and individuals will know and take their place. To others, these changes represent something quite different, a coming of wisdom, an ability to see farther than our predecessors, an unmasking of a reality that had been obfuscated for too long by a rhetoric of reform and benevolence.

But in effect, this description has only pushed the question back one stage. Why this loss of civitas? Or, alternately, why this new-found wisdom? We may well be too close to the issues to be able to formulate compelling hypotheses, but nevertheless, some of the elements promoting the change can be sketched. The bridge between the Progressive ideology and this new sense of things may well be the civil rights movement. In its origins, this movement was prototypically Progressive, its leaders confident that the attainment of equality for blacks would in no way conflict with the interest of society as a whole. Throughout the several decades of litigation that led up to the 1954 Supreme Court decision in *Brown* v. *Board of Education*, and down until 1966, the civil rights movement assumed that no basic clash of interests existed. Yes, some Southern bigots, the likes of bull-headed sheriffs, would lose out. But apart from the lunatic-fringe racists, there would be no victims.

The finest expression of this optimism came from Martin Luther King. And no speech of his, or perhaps more properly, no sermon of his, better captured this quality than his famous "I have a dream," delivered August 28, 1963. He spoke from the steps of the Lincoln Memorial; the band struck up the "Battle Hymn of the Republic" as he rose; and King opened appropriately enough with the words "Five score years ago." There was no need, King told his rapt audience, "to satisfy our thirst for freedom by drinking from the cup of bitterness and hatred." He went on: "Our white brothers . . . have come to realize that their destiny is tied up with our destiny and their freedom is inextricably bound to our freedom." "My dream," declared King, "is a dream deeply rooted in the American dream. I have a dream that one day on the red hills of Georgia the sons of former slaves and the sons of former slave owners will be able to sit down together at the table of brotherhood. . . . This is our hope. This is our faith. . . . With this faith we will be able to transform the jangling discords of our nation into a beautiful symphony of brotherhood." King ended his speech with the lines: "We will be able to speed up that day when all of God's children, black men and white men, Jews and Gentiles, Protestants and Catholics, will be able to join hands and sing in the words of the old Negro spiritual, Free at Last! Free at Last! Thank God almighty, we are free at last!"

It is almost embarrassing to read King's words today. Not only because we have fallen so far short of living up to his dream, but because his very announcement of his dream seems so very soft, so very tender, so very out of keeping with the realities of the world as we perceive them. Most dramatically, it is his notions of the possibility of brotherhood, or to put it into more mundane terms, the ability to satisfy at once the interests of everyone, that now seems so problematic. The turning point was probably 1966. After a series of impressive legislative victories, the civil rights movement met its first defeat that year—and the issue upon which it met its defeat is still very much with us today, the issue of open housing. 1966 was also the year that the formulations of "black power" first came to the fore. And black power, unlike King's rhetoric, looked first not to brotherhood, but to separatism; it premised itself not upon a mutuality of interests that all members of this society shared, but upon basic conflicts within this society. It announced in no uncertain terms that blacks had better organize themselves, get control of their own economic institutions, their own political institutions, their own community, if they would ever achieve substantial gains. And in all so many ways, the changeover from dreams of brotherhood to black power is paradigmatic of the changes that have transformed our society from 1966 until the present.

The ranks of black power may well have never amounted to more than a fraction of the black community. But far more important, black power became the strategy that every minority group in our society attempted to emulate. One finds this in the organization of welfare rights, with equal clarity, and with direct historical continuities, in the movements for prisoners' rights, mental patients' rights, the rights of the retarded, and the rights of children. The commonalities are clear: organize one's own special-interest group; press one's demands. The perspective is not the perspective of common welfare but the needs of the particular group. The intellectual premises are not unity but conflict. It is "us" versus "them."

In many ways, it was the dissatisfaction among blacks themselves with the advances made by the civil rights movement that helped generate this changed outlook. Rightly or wrongly, they believed that progress was too slow to come, that commonality of interests was not serving their own welfare. And that assumption, based upon the black experience, has fueled the various protest movements of other minority groups. So too, one should not minimize the implications of the changes in the American economy between the pre- and post-1965 period. The slowdown in economic growth that occurred after the mid-1960s, and the recessions that followed, to an extraordinary degree shook people's faith in the idea that an expanding economy would ultimately solve all of America's social problems. Added to this, of course, was a new concern for the allocation of scarce resources. Even before the oil shortages, conservationists and ecologists were warning us that our resources were finite and limited. And finally, every cynical judgment about the nature of American society seemed to be confirmed by the course of the Vietnam war. Here was a moment when a posture of "us" versus "them" seemed to make the best of sense.

One of the leading Progressive social planners, Charles Merriam of the University of Chicago, once wrote: "The most tragic moments in human life are those in which the value systems are unreconciled— when one cries out against another; the family against the state, the state against the church, the neighborhood against the distant capitol, life in the broader sense against non-life or narrow life—against the end of life." Merriam was ever thankful that his times, he believed, were not so tragic. No final conflict, he insisted, separated "self interest and the public interest." But in Merriam's sense of the term, we do indeed face tragedy. We can no longer entertain the simple hope that interests can be reconciled, that public interest and self-interest will necessarily coincide.

In light of this record and these prevailing assumptions, one can well appreciate how appealing and attractive a host of constituencies find a "liberty" model. Convinced that paternalistic state intervention in the

name of the common good has all too typically worked
to their disadvantage, they are now determined to rid
themselves of the onus of ostensibly protective and
benevolent oversight and substitute instead a commitment to their own autonomy. Thus, the emergence of
a series of liberation and rights movements, from
women's liberation to welfare rights. In all these cases
the goal is to reduce state power, to define the groups'
aims in terms of rights that should be immune from
interference, not needs that ought to be fulfilled. And
in many instances this strategy makes fundamental
good sense and does further the particular interests of
the group. Do not deprive us of our liberty to follow
our own life-styles because we are women, or ostensibly in need of treatment, or committed to a different
sexual orientation, or because we are young, or because we are poor. A liberty model is most effective
and appropriate in removing fetters that have blocked
freedom of choice and action.

But the expansion of rights solves only part of the
problem, for there do remain, like it or not, needs as
well, imbalances in economic and social power, in inherited physical constitutions, that demand redress. It
is not the goal of a liberty model to promote neglect,
to legitimate cruelty and inattention in the name of
rights. Rather, this camp recognizes that state intervention may often be necessary, but must take place
with a minimum of discretionary authority, with the
objects of protection or improvement having a deter-
minative voice in the shaping of the program itself. To
this end, advocates of the liberty model are far more
comfortable with an adversarial approach, an open
admission of conflict of interest, than with an equality
model with its presumption of harmony of interests.

In practice, such a commitment means that liberty-minded groups will advocate a clear delineation of the powers of the state, more prepared to trust to a political process that carefully spells out authority and responsibility than to an open-ended grant of authority to administrators to do as they please. Assuming that the players are competitive, that the game will be won by some and lost by others, it seems best to keep the rules clear, to know in advance how the action will proceed. So, better to list what welfare mothers are entitled to, rather than let the social worker act in her mysterious ways. Import all procedural protections into the juvenile court, rather than trust to the benevolence of its judge. Fix the terms for juvenile delinquents, make them consistent with adult ones, rather than allow the judge to pass indeterminate sentences that could stretch through the years of one's minority.

By the same token, better to trust to the skills of a lawyer in court than to the good intentions of the state or the agency or the institution. Presupposing conflict, let the battle be fought with both sides armed. Hence, the call for lawyers for children so that their wishes can be represented in custody cases, and their needs fully considered before they are institutionalized in the name of treatment. Hence, the call for lawyers inside the mental hospital, so that those diagnosed and committed as mentally ill will be fully informed of their rights and their ability to exercise choice expanded. Hence, the call for lawyers for students, so that their self-interest and not that of the high school or the college will be defended. And hence, the call for lawyers for welfare recipients and prisoners, so that their rights will be promoted, and the authority of social workers, probation officers, wardens, and guards will be reduced.

There is no denying that a liberty model and an

adversarial stance may pose as many questions as they solve about the problems of dependency in American society. For one, a focus on rights may well give a new legitimacy to neglect, allowing conservatives to join in the chorus for rights, not for the sake of maximizing choice but for reducing tax-based expenditures. For another, the traits of the lawyers are not those that would necessarily warm anybody's heart, let alone those who stand in need of support. It was Willard Gaylin who commented, with all sarcasm intended, that he finally understood the motive impulse of the adversarial movement: to substitute for the hard-nosed, belligerent, and tough-minded psychiatrist the attention of the gentle, understanding, empathetic lawyer! For still another, an adversarial model, setting interest off against interest, does seem to run the clear risk of creating a kind of ultimate shoot-out in which, by definition, the powerless lose and the powerful win. How absurd to push for confrontation when all the advantages are on the other side. Finally, courts are not the most reliable or consistent institutions to trust to in an effort to advance the claims of minorities. The new reformers themselves are fully aware of the grimmer prospects they face as the Warren Court gives way to the Burger Court.

But it is not the point of this essay to predict how a liberty model and adversarial tactics will fare in the future so much as to make clear how far the post-1960s reformers have moved from the Progressive tradition. The optimism and confidence that Progressives shared, both about the wisdom and potential effectiveness of their social policies, their firm sense of having diagnosed the problems of dependency and formulated the right programs to eliminate it, their belief in the superiority of their values and all that meant to their ability to define and to attempt to implement the proper life-styles in all citizens and classes, have disappeared and can hardly be resurrected. To try to recapture their vision of things, to assume as they did that the state should act as parent, is to misread in the most basic way the realities of our own particular social situation and to embark on a futile and probably dangerous endeavor.

Rather than trying to revive an older type of social contract, under which the better sort, the expert and the professional, was to act benevolently toward others and on their behalf, we would do better to address a very different series of issues. Will we as a society be able to recognize and respect rights and yet not ignore needs? Can we do good to others, but on their terms? Rather than wondering how professional expertise and discretionary authority can be exercised in the best interest of the client or the patient, we should ponder how the objects of authority can protect themselves against abuse without depriving themselves of the benefits that experts can deliver—and to turn the matter around in this way represents more than just a stylistic revision. Or to revert to the modern horror stories, is there some way that we can give Mrs. Lake her freedom and yet not breed cruelty? These are the right questions to be confronting, even if the record of American reform gives little reason to be confident that we will answer them well.

FURTHER READING

American attitudes toward dependency in the twentieth century are traced skillfully in Robert Bremner's *From the Depths: The Discovery of Poverty in the United States* (New York: New York University Press, 1956). Two excellent studies of the emergence of the reform activities are: Allen F. Davis, *Spearheads for Reform: The Social Settlements and the Progressive Movement* (New York: Oxford University Press, 1967); and Roy Lubove, *The Professional Altruist: The Emergence of Social Work as a Career, 1880–1930* (New York: Atheneum, 1969). To bring the story through the Depression decade, see Clarke Chambers, *Seedtime of Reform: American Social Service and Social Action* (Minneapolis: University of Minnesota Press, 1963); and Josephine C. Brown, *Public Relief, 1929–1939* (New York: Octagon, 1940). For astute analyses of the contemporary response to dependecy, begin with Richard Cloward and Francis Fox Piven, *Regulating the Poor: The Functions of Public Welfare* (New York: Pantheon Books, 1971); Elliot Liebow, *Tally's Corner* (Boston: Little, Brown, 1967); and Daniel P. Moynihan, ed., *On Understanding Poverty* (New York: Basic Books, 1969). For a more conservative perspective, see Edward Banfield, *The Unheavenly City* (Boston: Basic Books, 1970). For a collection of source materials, see David J. Rothman and Sheila M. Rothman, eds., *On Their Own: The Poor in Modern America* (Reading, Mass.: Addison-Wesley, 1972). Historians have concerned themselves less with delinquency than dependency. The nineteenth-century record is traced in David J. Rothman, *The Discovery of the Asylum* (Boston: Little, Brown, 1971). For the twentieth century, see Jack Holl, *Juvenile Reform in the Progressive Era* (Ithaca: Cornell University Press, 1971); and Anthony M. Platt, *The Child Savers: The Invention of Delinquency* (Chicago: University of Chicago Press, 1969).

PRISONERS OF BENEVOLENCE:

POWER VERSUS LIBERTY IN THE WELFARE STATE

Ira Glasser

THE QUESTIONS RAISED BY DAVID ROTHMAN AT the conclusion of his essay—can we respect rights and yet not ignore needs; can we allow for individual autonomy and yet fulfill social obligations—are not quite so novel as he suggests. While they are novel indeed as applied to the social programs of the Progressives, there is much precedent in American tradition prior to the Progressives for balancing the claims of individual liberty against the legitimate interests and obligations of society. In fact, the striking of such a balance through a written Constitution is probably a uniquely American response to the questions Rothman raises. That response was fashioned—primarily through the Bill of Rights—more than a century before the Progressives took hold, and reflected less innocence about and more fear of governmental power. The "rights movement" during the eighteenth century had little in common with the "needs movement" of the early twentieth century, and if we wish to answer Rothman's questions, it is to the eighteenth century that we must turn.

The Bill of Rights was devised to protect individual rights against the excesses of well-intentioned, democratically elected political rulers. Rights were defined rather simply as limits on government power. To say that a citizen had the *right* to distribute a leaflet or worship freely literally meant that the government was without the legal *power* to stop him.

Virtually every right was so defined. The right to be secure in one's own home from unreasonable government intrusion literally meant that not even the highest government official possessed the legal power to enter:

> The poorest man may in his cottage bid defiance to the crown. It may be frail—its roof may shake—the wind may enter—the rain may enter—but the King of England cannot enter—all his force dares not cross the threshold of the ruined tenement!*

"Over himself," wrote John Stuart Mill, "over his own body and mind, the individual is sovereign," and it was precisely to define and construct legal protections for personal sovereignty that the Bill of Rights was added to the fledgling United States Constitution in 1789.

For the early American colonists there was ample reason to construct such limits on governmental power. The Fourth Amendment to the Constitution, which sharply limited the power of government officials to search and seize individual citizens, was no abstract ideal invented by law professors in academic ivory towers, but rather the product of searing experience. During the fifteen years before the American Revolution, it was commonplace to be invaded in one's own home by British soldiers conducting unrestricted, house-to-house searches in order to enforce harsh tax laws and seize literature hostile to the Crown. Those searches—more feared at that time than burglars are feared today—created the political climate in which the Fourth Amendment

*William Pitt, Earl of Chatham.

and, indeed, the entire Bill of Rights was adopted.

In fact, the Bill of Rights, for all its grandeur, was not a very ambitious document. It sought not to bestow upon government the power to do good for people, but rather and more modestly sought to limit the government's power to do harm. The Bill of Rights focused not upon the good intentions of democratic rulers, but rather upon the harm to individual rights that might flow from their excesses. In fact, the Bill of Rights assumed their excesses and sought to limit them.

Most of the constitutional amendments establishing individual rights were written negatively: "Congress shall make no law . . . abridging the freedom of speech," says the First Amendment; "No person . . . shall be compelled in any criminal case to be a witness against himself," says the Fifth Amendment; "Nor shall any State deprive any person of life, liberty, or property without due process of law," says the Fourteenth.* These amendments say what government may *not* do. For those early Americans who believed that "governments are instituted" in part "to secure [individual] rights," it was not enough merely to enumerate the powers of government and assume that government officials would not exceed those powers. It was crucial, they believed, also to enumerate those powers that government officials should never be allowed to exercise.

Those who opposed the Bill of Rights believed such explicit limits were redundant and unnecessary. It was enough, they argued, to list the powers government would have and assume that no other powers would

*Although the Fourteenth Amendment was adopted nearly a century later, it continued to reflect the limiting language of the first ten.

inhere. Those who advocated the Bill of Rights were more fearful. If explicit limits on government power were not included, they argued, government officials would surely go beyond their enumerated powers. The Bill of Rights was the product of that fear.

The theory of politics that became encodified in the Constitution and the Bill of Rights was based on a particular view of the world as one that was anything but benign. The intellectual history of the decade before the Declaration of Independence is, as the Harvard historian Bernard Bailyn has written, "the story of the clarification and consolidation under the pressure of events of [this] view of the world. . . ." In a fascinating book called *Pamphlets of the American Revolution*, Bailyn describes this particularly American world view, and the theory of politics that emerged from it.*

For the prerevolutionary colonists, the ultimate explanation of every political controversy was the disposition of *power*. Power was defined as *dominion*—the dominion of some people over others, the human control of human life, ultimately force, ultimately compulsion.

The essential characteristic of power was its *aggressiveness*, what Bailyn calls "its endlessly propulsive tendency to expand itself beyond legitimate boundaries." In the pamphlets of the American Revolution, words like "trust" and "benevolence" cannot be found among the many descriptions of power. According to Bailyn, the metaphor most commonly used to express the colonists' view of power was the act of *trespassing*. Power was said to have "an encroaching

---

*The discussion that follows relies heavily upon, and often paraphrases, Bailyn's work.

nature," a pushing, grasping, *devouring* nature. It was said to be "tenacious," "like a cancer," "restless, aspiring and insatiable."

The natural prey of power, and its necessary victim, was liberty, or law, or right. The prerevolutionary writers saw the public world divided into two innately antagonistic spheres—power and liberty, the latter delicate, passive, above all *fragile.* "The one must be resisted, the other defended, and the two must never be confused."

Power was not itself evil, but it was *dangerous.* And power resided predominantly in the hands of government. Liberty was not—as it seems sometimes to be for us today—the concern and interest of all, governors and the governed alike; rather, liberty was the concern and interest only of the governed. "The wielders of power did not speak for it, nor did they naturally serve it. Their interest was to use and develop power, no less natural and necessary than liberty, but more dangerous."

This world view was not based on an abstract understanding of power, but rather on a practical understanding of people, and their "lust for self-aggrandizement." The point on which there was absolute agreement in those days was that people in general— as a species—were incapable of withstanding the temptations and seductions of power. Therefore, the protection of liberty—always vulnerable against the encroachments of power—required something more than faith in the decent intentions and kind instincts of people. For the early Americans knew that decent intentions and kind instincts could disappear—to use Dashiell Hammett's fetching image—like a fist disappears when you open your hand. And what would protect liberty then?

What was required to protect liberty were legal and political structures that, once erected, would be difficult to tear down. The prohibition of standing armies was one method of limiting governmental power; the direct distribution and fragmentation of power as set forth in the Constitution were another; and the Bill of Rights was a third. The mutual interest of all citizens in individual liberty was seen to derive precisely from the prevention of *dominion*, of too great a concentration of discretionary power. The constitutional separation of powers and the Bill of Rights were designed to create an inertia in favor of liberty that not even democratic majorities could overcome in moments of frenzy, or when the appetite for power grew too strong.

The maintenance of liberty was seen as a consistently hazardous business by the American colonists because of their view of human nature. No echo of Willard Gaylin's biological imperatives for decency and caring are to be found in their writings. For them, the public world, as distinct from the private world where Gaylin's imperatives might well reign, was a harsh and inhospitable place. The public waters were full of sharks.

No one seemed immune from this view of human nature, not even the most celebrated apostles of liberty. Even Thomas Jefferson, as Leonard Levy has pointed out,* was much less the civil libertarian *when he was president.*

Focusing on the darker side of Jefferson's commitment to liberty, and using that focus to illuminate the contradiction and limitations of libertarian leadership in the midst of power, Levy reminds us that

---

Jefferson and Civil Liberties: The Darker Side, Belknap Press, 1963.

Jefferson at one time or another supported loyalty oaths; countenanced internment camps for political suspects; drafted a bill of attainder; urged prosecutions for seditious libel; trampled on the Fourth Amendment; condoned military despotism; used the Army to enforce laws in time of peace; censored reading; chose professors for their political opinions; and endorsed the doctrine that the means, however odious, were justified by the ends.

Jefferson's lapses were in large part natural and to be expected. They "did not result from hypocrisy or meanness of spirit," but rather derived, in part, from the fact that many circumstances seemed to Jefferson to require the sacrifice of his libertarian ideals for "larger" and more compelling governmental ends.

Today, we may be surprised to learn of Jefferson's darker side, as we might be surprised to learn that the presidential order upon which John Mitchell relied to authorize his "national security" wiretaps was issued not by Richard Nixon but by Franklin Delano Roosevelt. But to the prerevolutionary writers, nothing Jefferson or any other president did would have been surprising. Their view of human nature predicted such outcomes: one should not confuse the province of liberty with the province of power, and those who exercise power should not be entrusted or expected to protect liberty: their self-restraint is a poor safeguard. Instead, power—no matter how benevolent of intention, no matter how libertarian in principle—must be restrained by law. Liberty requires, concludes Levy, that "the state must be bitted and bridled by a Bill of Rights . . . its protections not to be the playthings of momentary majorities or of those in power."

Thus the protection of individual liberty was seen as flowing from an *adversarial* process. Government was established by the consent of the governed, but government was nonetheless an adversary of the governed, and a dangerous one at that.

I. The Rise of Social Services: How Liberty Was Seduced and Ravaged by Good Intentions

In eighteenth-century America, "the government" consisted of the political institutions of the state; the individual whose liberty needed protection against those institutions was the citizen. Two hundred years later, as David Rothman's previous essay amply points out, "the government" has become much more than the political institutions of the state; it now also includes the social institutions of caring: public schools, mental hospitals, public housing authorities, developmental centers for the retarded, foster care agencies for homeless children, nursing homes for the aged, welfare agencies for the poor.

A common phrase—*social services*—arose to describe these institutions and they came to be widely perceived, especially by political liberals, as entirely humanitarian and benevolent, an undifferentiated and untroublesome *social* extension of humanity's best *individual* instincts. If it was natural—indeed imperative—for individuals to love and provide care for their infant children or those members of their family who had become helpless through age or other natural calamity, why then it was just as natural, and nearly as uncomplicated, for society to love and provide care for those who needed it and could not otherwise get it.

If there were problems with public social services,

they were largely problems of money. Liberal society, which is to say caring society, came mostly to believe that the only difficulty with social services was that there weren't enough to go around; the public sector, they argued, was being starved in the midst of private affluence. If the quality of public education, public housing, child care, medical care, and welfare was not what it should be, it was primarily because of inadequate resources. What was needed, according to the liberals, was more, not less, public intervention.

This undifferentiated view of social services, and the political context in which the struggle to provide social services took place, tended to blind liberals to certain unintended consequences of their good works. Because their motives were benevolent, their ends good, and their purpose caring, *they assumed the posture of parents* toward the recipients of their largesse. They failed utterly to resist the impulse toward paternalism, which in another context Bernard Bailyn called "the endlessly propulsive tendency" of power to expand itself and establish *dominion* over people's lives. They eagerly embraced such dominion and persuaded themselves that by doing so they were helping the helpless. Dominion became legitimate: those who managed social services—not infrequently liberals themselves—came to enjoy a degree of discretionary power over their clients that normally only parents are allowed over their children. As a result, they infantilized those they intended to help, and denied them their rights.

Not until the clients of service institutions rebelled in the 1960s did anyone begin to look with skepticism upon these good works. We all trusted the social services and did not fear service professionals. We built no legal restraints into the delivery systems of social services. We became oblivious, in the context of social services, to the adversarial relationship between power and liberty, and we assumed that the interests of clients were not in conflict with the interests of social service agencies. In fact, we adopted the fiction that the interests of clients were identical with the interests of social service agencies, a fiction we have not yet completely shed. The world view that the early Americans brought to their understanding of government was no part of our understanding of social services.

Vast discretionary power thus came to be vested in an army of civil servants, appointed by examination and organized into huge service bureaucracies, which began quietly and silently to trespass upon the private lives and rights of millions of citizens. If any of those citizens complained about such trespass, for a long time no one listened.

Many people, though decidedly not children, came routinely to depend, as if they were children, upon social services provided by the state for their daily sustenance, and sometimes for survival itself. From a direction wholly unanticipated by the early Americans, government power thus came to touch millions of people heavily, and in ways that clearly violated the Bill of Rights. Sometimes the violations were substantial, and the intrusions nearly total. Consider the example of nursing homes.

Most of the relatively recent public debate over nursing homes has concentrated upon the poor quality of care provided, or upon fiscal fraud. Somewhat obscured has been the quality of life that results from institutional pressures inherent even in "good" nursing homes, when the interests of the home conflict with the interests of the patient. For example, the nursing home may have an interest—a legitimate interest—in getting paid for the services it provides, which should disqualify it from being an impartial protector of the aged person's assets. Nonetheless, nursing homes often control the assets of their patients and manipulate those assets to their own ends and to the detriment of their patients. Similarly, the patient may desire the freedom to come and go, to socialize, to have visitors and activities, to retain privacy, while the home's interests may run more to administrative convenience and order. When such conflicts of interest arise, the nearly parental powers of the nursing home can quickly suffocate the basic rights of individual patients.

As a result, many nursing home patients find themselves in a desperate position, stripped of power and desolate of dignity. They are, most of them, competent in the eyes of the law. They have not been convicted of any crime, or adjudged insane or a danger to themselves or others. They are not children. They are adults and are presumed competent. Their rights and freedoms cannot legally be denied through any *ad hoc* informal decisions by nursing home officials or even by well-meaning family members.

Yet despite their legal status as free citizens, nursing home patients share much with children, mental patients, and even prisoners. The control of individual life in nursing homes is pervasive. The elderly person is dependent upon the institution for food, clothing, medical care, recreation, companionship—in short, for all the physical and emotional elements of survival. The home exercises complete discretionary power over the aged person. It decides whether the patient is capable of receiving mail, or of handling spending money. It decides whether the patient can walk in the neighborhood. It decides who will be allowed to visit the patient and when. It decides whether the patient shall stay or leave.*

The discretionary power faced by the aged in nursing homes also has traditionally been faced by residents of other service institutions, such as patients in mental hospitals, or children in foster care institutions. Such residents also have much in common with soldiers in the army and convicts in prison. In fact, perhaps the best way to appreciate the degree of control in such service institutions is to compare them to the

---

*Nursing homes are not directly run by the government. However, that does not mean that they are any less public institutions. Whenever the government undertakes an obligation, e.g., to provide education at public expense, to provide care for foster children at public expense, or to provide care for the elderly at public expense, it normally does so in one of two ways: either the public service is provided directly through public institutions like schools, or it is provided indirectly through public subsidies as in the case of nursing homes or child-care agencies. Such public subsidies may come in the form of medicaid payments or direct payments on a contractual basis from the government to the institution for each person served. Normally, there are government restrictions on how such payments may be used, and the "private" agency becomes an agent of the government. In the latter instances, the government discharges its obligation through such "private" agencies, but it is still a government-provided service. So-called voluntary child-care agencies, for example, commonly receive 80 to 100 percent of their *entire* budgets from public funds for providing services to foster children that the state is legally obligated to provide. These agencies, and the programs they run, are in no sense private. Similarly, the notion that nursing homes are private institutions entering into private contracts with individual patients is a convenient fiction. In fact, nursing homes are the instrument through which the government discharges its obligation to take care of the elderly, and the pattern of government funding leaves individual patients little freedom to "contract" or to choose. Nursing homes are heavily supported—in many cases totally supported—by public funds through state and federal medicare payments. Such public funds are not available, in anything even remotely like similar amounts, directly to the aged and their families to be used to sustain older people in their own homes. Instead, such public funds are available only to institutions like nursing homes and are made available without regulatory strings attached that could limit the discretionary powers of the homes to intrude so pervasively upon their patients and violate their rights. Nursing homes should therefore be viewed, for purposes of this discussion, as essentially another government institution.

military and to prisons. In each, every detail of an inmate's life is potentially open for scrutiny and inspection. It often begins with the very process of admission:

> . . . taking a life history, photographing, weighing, fingerprinting, assigning numbers, searching, listing personal possessions for storage, undressing, bathing, disinfecting, hair-cutting, issuing institutional clothing, instructing as to rules, and assigning to quarters.*

The new arrival is thus "shaped and coded into an object that can be fed into the administrative machinery of the establishment, to be worked on smoothly by routine operations." Afterward there are various other "abasements, degradations, humiliations and profanations of self": meaningless make-work, denial of sex, forced deference, penalties for self-expression, unfair procedures. The entire process resembles nothing so much as basic training in the military, the purpose of which is concededly to abolish individuality. The reach of the institution extends to the most personal aspects of one's life, and significantly to aspects that are meaningless to anyone else—to dress, to style, to personal appearance and deportment. In the military, the function of such dominion is undisputed: if you can control the personal details of someone's life, if you can impose your institutional will even upon personal appearance, then you can control everything —how he thinks, how he acts, how he responds to orders. However appropriate such control might be in the military, it is hard to justify within caring institutions. Yet, typically, inmates of such institutions have been subjected to precisely such personal controls. In the end, Erving Goffman tells us, "[t]he inmate cannot

*Asylums, Erving Goffman, Anchor Press, 1961, p. 16.

easily escape from the press of judgmental officials and from the enveloping tissue of constraint."*

Nor has this "tissue of constraint" been limited to residential service institutions like nursing homes or mental hospitals. Similar intrusions flowing from similar discretionary powers were also to be found, though to lesser degrees, in the administration of public schools, public housing, and public welfare. For a long while, no one thought to question such intrusions or to limit the discretionary powers of public servants providing social services to the needy. Violations of individual rights that would have created an instantaneous political and legal clamor had they been perpetrated by the police went unrecognized when they were perpetrated by social service professionals. Because such professionals were presumed to be acting in "the best interests" of their "clients," no one thought to question the excesses of their power. They were not cops.

In fact, they were more like parents. (How could a parent, looking through a child's belongings, be accused of an illegal search? How could a parent, demanding deference, determining a child's bedtime, telling him what clothes to wear, punishing him for "talking back," or even hitting him, be accused of violating constitutional rights?) In some institutions, service professionals actually and explicitly claimed the legal powers of surrogate parents. In schools, for example, teachers and principals tried to justify their discretionary power over students by the doctrine of *in loco parentis*. According to this doctrine, parents—just by sending their children to school—delegate their powers to school officials, who are then permit-

*Goffman, *ibid*.

ted to act in the place of the parent. Child-care agencies literally and legally assumed complete parental powers over their wards. Under certain conditions, so did mental hospitals and nursing homes. Other services, like public housing, often treated their clients like children, even without claiming the legal power of surrogate parents.

And so a tradition grew up. The Bill of Rights existed, but it did not apply to service institutions. It limited the powers of elected representatives, political officials, and the police, but it did not limit the powers of high school principals, social workers, housing officials, or mental health professionals. Those citizens who lived under the jurisdiction of the service professionals were consequently without rights. Students in school, the poor in public housing, the sick in mental hospitals, the aged in nursing homes, and the young in foster care institutions all came to resemble each other in a strange and critical way. All were enmeshed against their wills in institutions ostensibly designed to benefit them. All were forced to waive their rights as a condition of receiving benefits. Students were required to go to school for their own benefit, children were sent to reformatories for "rehabilitation," and the aged and erratic were committed to mental "hospitals" to "get well," or to nursing "homes" to receive "care." Welfare fed and clothed the poor, and public housing provided shelter. But individual rights became unthinkable.

For people who needed shelter, the government provided public housing. But admission was denied for reasons such as poor housekeeping, irregular work history, frequent separations of husband and wife, single-parent families, common-law marriages, lack of furniture, apparent mental retardation, dishonorable discharge from the military, or the arrest of one's child. These standards were not the result of *ad hoc* decisions by unfair individuals; they were actually written down as the legal regulations of public housing authorities, and they gave housing officials unprecedented discretion—the early Americans would have called it *dominion*—over other people's lives. Private troubles became a reason for public punishment.

For people who needed money, the government provided welfare. But eligibility standards depended on morality. Every detail of a recipient's life was subject to scrutiny. Women were allowed different numbers of sanitary napkins each month, and men different numbers of razor blades, depending on whether they were employed or not. The same distinction governed the number of times one could have one's coat cleaned. There were no allowances for newspapers, and telephones were considered a luxury, even for the blind. A single woman with preschool, dependent children could have her children's benefits revoked if she were found to be sleeping with a man, and midnight raids by caseworkers became a common method of discovering such behavior. The abolition of privacy became a condition of survival.

For children in trouble and whose families did not have the resources to help, the government provided "services" through a system of family courts. Punishment was no part of the purpose of these courts, whose only function was to rehabilitate. But services that might have been purchased if a child's family was affluent enough—a governess, a tutor, a psychologist, a special school, a homemaker—were not provided. Instead, children were removed from their families and incarcerated, like criminals and often together with criminals, for truancy, for running away from home, for staying out too late, for using bad language, for sexual promiscuity, or for vague reasons like disobedience or incorrigibility. Whatever their problems, they did not usually come out of those institutions better off than they had been when they entered, or even than they might have been if they had been left alone. If their families had begun to break up under the pressure of poverty, the government's intervention often accelerated the breakup and made it permanent.

In institutions of lesser powers, like public schools, intrusions and degradations were nonetheless substantial. Codes of dress and personal appearance were enforced with disproportionate intensity, as if the structure of public education itself would crumble if a boy were allowed another quarter-inch of hair or a girl were permitted to wear slacks. Freedom of speech was forbidden. While students were taught to revere James Madison and the First Amendment in their social studies classes, they were swiftly suspended for extending those lessons to their own lives. Other students were suspended for truancy: their problem was that they were not attending school enough, and the school "helped" by not permitting them to attend at all. All of these actions were taken unfairly, without giving the banished student an opportunity to explain or contest the suspension. Fair hearings were not necessary because everyone had the student's best interests at heart. Arbitrariness became the concomitant of benevolence.

During the 1960s, many of these groups began to challenge the extraordinary powers of their benefactors. Buttons appeared on the collars of New York City high school students that proclaimed "Free the New York 275,000"; groups like the National Welfare Rights Organization and the Mental Patients Liberation Front arose; unions were organized in prisons. By the mid-1970s the movement was in full flower. In Syracuse, New York, a poster looking much like a traditional March of Dimes poster began to circulate, its legend announcing a new stance toward charity: "You Gave Us Your Dimes. Now We Want Our Rights."

The new rights movements displayed all the accoutrements of orthodox political organization. There were meetings, rallies, leaflets, and newspapers. Often the response of the service professionals was unexpectedly repressive. Students peacefully handing out leaflets or homemade "underground" newspapers were suspended for distributing "seditious" literature, while welfare rights advocates were arrested for handing out eligibility information to recipients in welfare centers. Not coincidentally, but at the same time, prisoners were being placed in solitary confinement for entries in their diary critical of prison officials and soldiers were being court-martialed for criticizing the war in Vietnam. The analogy between service institutions on the one hand and the military and prisons on the other remained consistent.

Procedural rights were also denied. People were suspended from school, evicted from public housing, denied welfare benefits, or committed to mental hospitals for arbitrary reasons or without the slightest semblance of due process or a fair opportunity to tell their side of the story.

Individual social service employees who tried to defend their clients against these substantive and procedural depredations quickly discovered the adversarial nature of charity. If they persisted in defending their clients, they were often fired. Fighting for clients' interests became too risky, and not many took the risk. Clients learned that, with few exceptions, they could not rely upon those who served them. So they began to rely upon themselves. Encouraged by the expansiveness of the Warren Court, and the explosive availability of civil rights, civil liberties, and poverty lawyers, client groups began to sue their benefactors. One by one during the 1960s all these groups went to court to establish the principle that the Bill of Rights applied to them, and to limit the powers of those who governed their lives. The response of service professionals was almost always the same: they resisted attempts to place limits on their discretion, and they felt betrayed by those they had sought to serve.

School principals claimed that without the unfettered discretion to suspend they could not maintain adequate discipline in the schools. Family court judges argued that it was necessary to "search" a welfare mother's house without a warrant in order to find out if her child was being abused. The New York State Department of Social Services supported solitary confinement in children's institutions as necessary to the overall rehabilitative purposes of confinement. Housing officials defended evictions of entire families by claiming that such evictions were necessary to protect other residents. Psychiatrists in Florida justified the fifteen-year incarceration, without treatment, of a nondangerous "patient" in a mental "hospital" by claiming, in effect, that incarceration itself was therapeutic. (They called it "milieu therapy.") In April 1977, the United States Supreme Court ruled that the beating of schoolchildren by teachers was not unconstitutional. A spokesman for the American Federation of Teachers hailed the ruling by defending teachers' discretion and by emphasizing their benevolent intentions: "I shudder," he said, "that people will say that we are Nazis who want to beat up kids. That's not it; teachers want to maintain a healthy atmosphere and they need *options*" (emphasis added). Another teacher spokesman added, "Teachers want corporal punishment retained as an option. *No one likes to see their options limited*"* (emphasis added).

Such justifications are not in principle different from those offered by the police. They, too, constantly clamor to be free of restrictions that they perceive as hampering them in their ability to do their job. Yet it is precisely those restrictions that define our rights. From the police point of view it might be easier to search whenever and whomever they want, and not be forced to obtain a warrant and convince a judge that their intended search is both reasonable and lawful. Yet our Constitution recognizes—and nearly everyone agrees—that such unlimited police discretion would come at the expense of citizens' rights. Similarly, unlimited professional discretion—whether the professional is a teacher, a social worker, a housing official, or a psychiatrist—comes at the expense of the client's rights.

Yet until the rights revolution of the sixties, no one saw it that way. Most professionals defended their own discretionary power—*and therefore opposed the rights of their clients*—with variations on the following argument:

1. I provide an essential and benevolent service. I am a helping professional: I teach, I heal, I rehabilitate, I provide shelter.

The New York Times, April 25, 1977, p. 24.

2. In order to provide my service well, it is necessary that I be allowed wide discretion. I am an expert. I know how to run schools, hospitals, children's shelters, housing programs, and I must be left alone to apply my special knowledge.

3. The adversary process is inappropriate to the service I provide. Lawyers are an intrusion. They don't have my expertise; they don't know how to run a specialized institution. The very notion of legal rights hampers my ability to provide my service effectively. The Bill of Rights is disruptive. How can I get on with the difficult business of teaching if I am forced constantly to justify my actions to lawyers at hearings? How can I protect a helpless child from physical abuse if I am not allowed access to the home without having to go before a judge and get a warrant?

This attitude received the highest legal endorsement in a case that reached the United States Supreme Court in late 1970. The case involved a woman, Barbara James, who was receiving welfare money for her dependent child, and who was notified that her home would be visited by a caseworker. Mrs. James offered to supply relevant information to welfare officials, but refused to permit the caseworker to "visit" her home. As a result, welfare aid to her children was terminated.

Mrs. James sued in federal court. She argued that the "visit" was a euphemism for a search, and said that the government had no legal power to search her home. The Fourth Amendment to the United States Constitution, she said, gave her the right to refuse such "visits." But the United States Supreme Court disagreed. Why?

In colonial America, British revenue officers had the power to search houses for smuggled goods. Colonial fears of such searches led to the Fourth Amendment

to the Constitution, which prohibits general searches
and narrowly limits search warrants except under
very special and particular conditions. In full, the
Fourth Amendment reads as follows:

> The rights of the people to be secure in their persons,
> houses, papers, and effects, against unreasonable
> searches and seizures, shall not be violated, and no
> warrants shall issue, but upon probable cause, sup-
> ported by Oath or affirmation, and particularly de-
> scribing the place to be searched, and the persons or
> things to be seized.

In practice, the Fourth Amendment means that the
police cannot just come into your house on the basis
of a general suspicion and rummage around. They
must have good cause to believe that a crime has been
committed, and that evidence of that crime is in the
place they want to search. They must be able to describe that evidence and why they think it is there. In
other words, they pretty much have to know what
they are looking for. And even if they do, it is not
enough to convince a superior police officer. Because
the unfettered discretion of police power can lead to
abuse, the decision to search may not be left to the
police. They have to convince a judge first, and he
must issue a warrant.

So if Barbara James had resisted an effort by the
police to enter her apartment she would have been
successful. And, in fact, the first court to hear her case
ruled in her favor. But in a 5–4 decision, the United
States Supreme Court ruled that the caseworker's visit
was not constitutionally the same as a police officer's
search. In what may go down as a classic line in the
history of Supreme Court phrases, Justice Harry
Blackmun ruled that "the caseworker is not a sleuth,

but rather, we trust, is a friend to one in need." That the "one in need" had come before the Court to claim the right to reject such "friendship" seemed lost on Justice Blackmun and the four other justices who voted with him.

A closer reading of Justice Blackmun's opinion makes it plain that he was able to draw such an easy distinction between welfare workers and cops only because of his belief, yes, even his faith, that welfare workers meant well, while the police were rightly to be feared. The caseworker's "primary objective," wrote Blackmun, "is, or should be, the welfare, not the prosecution, of the aid recipient for whom the worker has profound responsibility."

Nor was the Court moved by the testimony of a dozen other welfare recipients, who said that caseworkers often come without notice or appointment, that such surprise visits can be "very embarrassing to me . . . when I have company" and that caseworkers sometimes ask "very personal questions" in front of children. None of this mattered. Bound by the vision of the benevolent purpose of welfare, the Court failed to see the violation of rights which, in a police context, even the Burger Court would have been quick to see and quick to stop.

As it turned out, the caseworker was not the guardian of his client's liberty. His province was power, and he exercised it. Her province was dependence, and she was forced to suffer the deprivation of her right to privacy. Because the discretionary power of the government was not limited by the Constitution, Barbara James's right was swept away. The early Americans might not have been surprised. To them, it might have seemed like just another governmental trespass.

Of course, Barbara James could have stopped the unwarranted government searches anytime: all she had to do was decline to accept welfare payments for her dependent children. In one federal lawsuit in Washington, D.C., a judge actually made that argument: a welfare recipient, he ruled, has "a perfect right to slam the door in the face of the investigator. Of course, he runs the risk then of being cut off the rolls." Residents of public housing, students in public schools, children in foster care institutions, patients in mental hospitals, and the aged in nursing homes faced similar "choices." Families in public housing could avoid official surveillance of their private affairs by leaving—except that they could not afford to leave. Students in public schools could avoid restrictions upon their personal appearance and freedom of political expression by leaving—except that they were compelled to attend or pay steeply for private schooling. Children in foster care institutions, patients in mental hospitals, and the aged in nursing homes often did not enjoy even that bleak alternative: incarcerated against their will, they could not avoid violations of their rights even by leaving.

These forms of dependence, of powerlessness really, are crucially different from the dependence and powerlessness we all face as infants. As infants, most of us are loved. "To be helpless," Willard Gaylin tells us earlier in this volume, "is not necessarily to be in jeopardy. To be helpless *and unloved* is the matrix of disaster." And although it is normal for parents to love their children, it is not normal for society to love the socially helpless. Who loves the aged, the mentally ill, or the troubled children of the poor? Who loves welfare recipients or the residents of public housing? Abstractly, perhaps, society adopts a superficially charitable attitude toward these groups. But if one looks at what society does, and not at what it says, there is little love reflected. The record of public charity is an unloving record of punishment, degradation, humiliation, intrusion, and incarceration. If parents treated their children the way society treats the helpless, they would be cited for neglect and child abuse. The power of "lovability," which normally saves the child from disaster, has no precise social analogue.

The varieties of social dependence, described in Dickens's novels and intrinsic to the modern American welfare state, have therefore resulted in profound violations of individual liberty. These violations were not explicitly anticipated by those who wrote our Constitution and its Bill of Rights. Dependence upon the institutions of caring establishes —for millions of people—a condition of fragility against encroachments of power, and benevolence is the mask that hides it. It is not that benevolence is itself mischievous or cynically to be regarded with mistrust. It is not benevolence we should abandon, but rather the naive faith that benevolence can mitigate the mischievousness of power so feared by those who wrote our Bill of Rights. We have traditionally been seduced into supposing that because they represented charity, service professionals could speak for the best interests of their clients. By now we should know better. Power is the natural antagonist of liberty, even if those who exercise power are filled with good intentions. Politically, we were not safe from the excesses of even so libertarian a man as Thomas Jefferson; socially, we are not safe from the excesses of our service institutions. Just as the liberty interests of the governed cannot be the concern of their governors, so the

liberty interests of the needy cannot be the concern of their benefactors. They both mean to govern well, *but they mean to govern*. They therefore
must be "bitted and bridled by a Bill of Rights."

It follows that we should respond to the claims of
service professionals as if they were cops. The caseworker whose job would be easier if he or she were
allowed unwarranted access to an individual's home is
no different from the police officer whose job would
also be easier if such access were allowed.

Both serve important social ends, but both are
dangerous. Both will violate rights in the course of
their jobs if they think it is important enough, *and
therefore that is a decision that cannot be left to
them.* They must, no less than Congress or the president or the FBI, be legally limited in exercising their
discretion.

We know who the cops are; we should at last know
who the service professionals are: not the guardians of
their clients' liberty.

II. Liberty in the Welfare State: The Doctrine of Least Harm

If it is economic inequity that causes many of the
forms of dependence we have discussed, and the
coerced waiver of rights such dependence often
produces, then it would seem to follow that the
way to remedy the loss of rights caused by economic dependence is to restructure society,
economically and politically, in order to eradicate
economic inequity. While such a goal is commendable and ought devoutly to be pursued, it begs the
immediate question and tends to be a convenient

way for the rest of us to avoid the problems that face the socially dependent *now*.

There are two reasons why the pursuit of economic equality is not a sufficient response to the problems we have discussed. First, even if it were possible within our finite future to attain a sufficient measure of economic equality, not all the forms of social dependence we have discussed would fade away. Infants in the biological family are not the only people who face what Willard Gaylin has called "intrinsic" dependence. Old people can become physically helpless too. Certain severely handicapped people and the profoundly retarded can be as necessarily dependent as infants. So can certain of the chronically ill. Poverty is not the only condition that can create classes of people who are socially dependent, though poverty clearly intensifies such dependence. Regardless of the degree to which we can one day successfully eliminate those forms of dependence that are purely, or dominantly, caused by economic inequity, we will always have within our midst significant numbers of dependent people who must be cared for by society. The perhaps unintended terrors and oppressions we seem to inflict upon such people as we care for them, and which they, because they are dependent, cannot avoid, must be remedied by means other than the effort to achieve economic equality.

Second, no one supposes we will attain a sufficient measure of economic equality within the lifetimes of those who currently suffer because they are dependent, or within the lifetimes of the next few generations. It is fundamentally cruel to avoid the pursuit of other remedies for the degradations suffered by the dependent, on the ground that such remedies will somehow make more distant the day when "fundamental" solutions are finally achieved. Those who can afford to postpone relatively modest remedies, because they are not suffering, in the hope of achieving more fundamental economic change, ought not to impose their abstract solutions upon those who are dependent today, and likely to continue to be dependent tomorrow.

It may well be analytically correct to distinguish between the "intrinsically" dependent (those who, like children, are dependent for natural causes that cannot be remedied) and the "extrinsically" dependent (those who, like welfare recipients, residents of public housing, foster children, or many of the old or mentally ill, have their dependence imposed upon them by economic insufficiency that presumably could be remedied in a just society). But if we care about the extrinsically dependent and want to avoid the paternalism that infantilizes them and strips them of their rights, we are constrained to ignore that analytic distinction and act as if "extrinsic" dependence were as natural as "intrinsic" dependence. Certainly, it is as consistent a social phenomenon.

The analytic distinction between "intrinsic" and "extrinsic" dependence may be crucial for the purpose of pursuing economic equality; it is useless, and even an obstacle, for the purpose of maintaining the liberty, the personal autonomy, the dignity, and the rights of the dependent against the depredations of their benefactors. It is the latter purpose—more modest, perhaps, but, like the Bill of Rights, ambitious enough—that occupies the remainder of this small essay. As Steven Marcus concluded earlier in this volume, "We can degrade people by caring for them, and we can degrade them by not caring for them." Our task is to identify and implement a set of principles that will continue to permit social programs of caring, but that will sharply limit their unintended, and often disastrous, consequences.* In this respect, we welcome social programs of caring, but recognize their dangers and seek to limit them, much as the early Americans welcomed a powerful democratic government, but feared its excesses and sought to limit them.

First Principle: The Bill of Rights applies to social institutions of caring and limits the powers of those institutions and their employees over the lives of the dependent.

The assumption of benevolence must be seen as an insufficient reason to grant unlimited discretionary power to service professionals. We must begin, at least legally, to mistrust service professionals as well as depend on them, much as we do the police. The legal fiction endorsed by Justice Blackmun and the Supreme Court in the case of Barbara James must finally and completely disappear.

To some extent, this principle has already been generally established, though much remains to be done. During the decade between the mid-1960s and the mid-1970s, an immense amount of litigation took place challenging the discretion of service institutions and

*That such principles, if implemented, are likely to have their own unintended, and perhaps unfortunate, consequences, I have no doubt. Therefore, though I believe the principles I shall suggest to be substantially self-limiting (like the Bill of Rights), they should as well be subjected to scrutiny and monitoring in order to minimize their unintended consequences. However, that task is beyond the scope of this essay, and perhaps beyond the capacity of its author, whose posture toward and experience with the social institutions of caring has inclined him in a certain direction, no less than the early Americans were inclined toward the political institutions of government.

seeking to establish particular rights for dependent individuals. Though some of it was unsuccessful, many new rights were secured, and unprecedented limits were imposed on institutions. This essay is hardly the occasion for setting forth a complete docket of such litigation, but it is useful to cite a few examples.

Students in public schools established their right to freedom of expression inside the school. In a landmark decision, the United States Supreme Court overturned the suspension of several teenage students who had publicized their objections to the war in Vietnam by wearing black armbands to school.* The Court ruled that students do not lose their First Amendment right to free expression when they enter school, and explicitly rejected the claim that school officials ought to continue to have the discretion to prohibit such expression. Other courts applied the same principle to different forms of expression, including newspapers, leaflets, buttons, and political clubs.

In a later decision, the Supreme Court also ruled that a student has the right to a fair hearing any time he is suspended from school.** The Court established that right by limiting the discretion of school officials to take away or suspend the student's entitlement to public education without adhering to the minimum procedures required by the Constitution to guarantee fairness. The traditional claim of school officials that such procedures were not necessary because they had the student's best interests at heart was rejected. Limits were placed on their discretion despite their good intentions.

Welfare recipients established many major new

---

*Tinker v. Des Moines Independent Community School District, 393 U.S. 503 (1969).

**Goss v. Lopez, 419 U.S. 565 (1975).

rights that restricted the discretion of social service officials to determine or revoke benefits and intrude upon their private lives. In one case, the Supreme Court ruled that welfare officials could not revoke benefits to needy children because their mother had sexual relations with an unrelated male.* In another case, the Court limited official discretion by ruling that welfare benefits could not be revoked without a prior fair hearing.** In a third, the Court prohibited local welfare officials from denying benefits to current residents who were otherwise eligible because they had not been residents for at least one year.† And even though, in the Barbara James case, the Supreme Court said that compulsory home visits did not require a search warrant, welfare officials were stopped by federal courts in other cases from conducting "unreasonable searches," such as the infamous midnight raids to detect women sleeping with unrelated men.

In housing, federal courts said that "the existence of an absolute and uncontrolled discretion in an agency of government vested with the administration of a vast program such as public housing would be an intolerable invitation to abuse," and ruled that constitutional standards of due process required public housing authorities to select tenants according to "ascertainable standards" and fair procedures.††

In juvenile justice, the Supreme Court established that "the Bill of Rights is [not] for adults only." In a case involving a minor from Arizona accused of making a lewd telephone call to a neighbor, the Court

---

*King v. Smith, 392 U.S. 309 (1968).
**Goldberg v. Kelly, 397 U.S. 254 (1970).
†Shapiro v. Thompson, 394 U.S. 618 (1969).
††Holmes v. New York City Housing Authority, 398 F.2d 262 (2d Cir. 1968); Escalera v. New York City Housing Authority, 425 F.2d 853 (2d Cir. 1970), cert. denied, 400 U.S. 853 (1970).

ruled that when a child faces a loss of liberty, he is entitled to a lawyer, notice of charges, the right to cross-examine witnesses, and the right to remain silent. All those rights had been denied by the Arizona juvenile court on the ground that juvenile courts were not strictly courts, but rather were more informal tribunals whose purpose was not to punish the accused minor, but to help him. The Supreme Court explicitly rejected such intended benevolence as a sufficient justification for the denial of constitutional rights.* A few years later, another federal court struck down a statute that authorized reformatory sentences of up to four years for minors who had committed acts for which the maximum sentence was one year if committed by an adult. The government had claimed that the longer sentence for juveniles was justified because it was not intended to punish, but rather to rehabilitate, and more time was required for rehabilitation. The court explicitly rejected that claim.** Similarly, another court later declared unconstitutional a statute authorizing incarceration of so-called wayward minors for the ostensible purpose of psychological and medical treatment. "Unbridled discretion," quoted the court, "however benevolently motivated, is frequently a poor substitute for principle and procedure."†

Though cases like these only established partial limits on the discretion of institutions, leaving many rights still unprotected, they did make it clear that the mere claim of benevolence was no longer sufficient to gain exemption from the limits imposed by the Bill of

---

*In re Gault, 387 U.S. 1 (1967).

**United States ex rel. Sero v. Preiser, 500 F.2d 1115 (2d Cir. 1974), cert. denied, 95 S. Ct. 1587 (1975).

†Gesicki v. Oswald, 336 F. Supp. 371 (S.D.N.Y. 1971).

Rights. Prison officials, mental health officials, and child-care officials also saw their discretion limited during those years, though on varying matters and in varying degrees. It would be fair to characterize the results of such litigation as a legal revolution, but it would be inaccurate to suggest that the revolution is anywhere near completed. Many institutions, or aspects of institutions, remain largely free of legal restrictions, and therefore the rights of individuals subject to the powers of those institutions do not exist or are in jeopardy.

Nursing homes provide one ready example of an institution still substantially untouched by the rights movement. Six important rights that do not now exist for nursing home patients are illustrative of what yet needs to be accomplished:*

1. *The right to control personal property.* Unless residents of total institutions can exercise control over their personal property, they will be at the mercy of the institution. Without the right to control personal property, the liberty of nursing home patients cannot exist.

This principle has recently been adopted by a federal court in Pennsylvania with respect to mental patients. There, the patients successfully challenged Pennsylvania's practice of applying patient resources to the cost of their care without any prior notice or hearing. Similarly, in New York, individuals adjudged to be mentally incompetent must be afforded a hearing before their right to control property can be transferred to a committee. These principles should also be applicable to aid the elderly to protect their resources

---

*The following discussion relies heavily on the work of Professor Sylvia Law of New York University Law School.

from attachment by either a nursing home or the state, but they commonly are not.

Often, an elderly person's sole or primary source of income is Social Security. Yet it is not unusual for Social Security checks to be automatically endorsed over to the nursing home or the state as a condition of continued care. Letters containing Social Security checks are segregated from other mail, sometimes opened, and personally delivered to patients with coercive instructions to endorse. Though the right to receive first-class mail without interference is constitutionally protected even against the CIA, Postal Service regulations appear to give institutional authorities complete control over delivery of mail to patients.

There is therefore little to prevent a nursing home from receiving full payment for the care provided an individual and, at the same time, coercing the individual to sign over Social Security checks or other resources to the home. Another more sophisticated version of this problem arises where a home makes extra charges for so-called supplemental services, beyond the basic services required by law. For example, a home may state that it provides a beauty parlor service, and then attach a patient's resources for payment for the service of washing the individual's hair.

Another important patient property interest is the right to privacy. Perhaps the most poignant loss suffered by nursing home residents is the loss of self, which results from a thorough stripping away of privacy. Nursing home residents should have a guaranteed place to keep their personal belongings. The disappearance of personal property is endemic in nursing homes, which are not now legally liable for lost property. Residents should also be protected in their right to close their doors to the watchful eyes of home administrators, and to the often alien assault of noise by staff, particularly from radios played loudly. Finally, most nursing homes make private contact between members of the opposite sex impossible, perhaps the most degrading intrusion of all.

2. *The right to control your own body.* The general law of torts, which basically regards as an assault any medical procedure carried out on an individual against his will, has been expanded to include the individual's right to receive all relevant information he would want to know before consenting to medical treatment. The tort law has thus been a vehicle for defining and enforcing the right to informed consent.

For nursing home patients, who often live in relative isolation, and who frequently are assaulted by the gross overuse and misuse of prescription drugs, the right to informed consent is crucial. Yet few, if any, cases raising a claim of informed consent on behalf of a nursing home patient can be found. In part, that is because tort cases normally are brought for money damages by malpractice attorneys working on a contingency-fee basis. There are simply no lawyers available to vindicate these rights for elderly residents of nursing homes.

3. *The right to come and go freely.* Since nursing home residents are, generally, competent adults, they are entitled to the same rights to freedom from restraint as other citizens. Hence the nursing home resident's claim to freedom from bodily restraint is fundamentally different from that of convicted prisoners or even of young children. Nursing home residents should have the right to come and go as they please, but they do not. Neither physical nor pharmaceutical restraints should be used except perhaps for brief periods during real emergencies. There have been virtually no cases litigating this right.

4. *The rights to free speech, association, petition,*

and counsel. The rights of speech, association, and petition are essential to nursing home residents. These rights would enable residents to band together to seek improvement in conditions in the home and to support one another. The organized association of inmates seeking their rights has proved critical to the securing of those rights in each and every other total institution. Indeed, the organization of various victim groups has been without exception the prerequisite to effective litigation by public-interest law firms. As a practical matter the organization of nursing home residents will probably not come into existence or long survive unless they have access to friends, organizers, lawyers, and others on the outside. Homes frequently attempt to limit visitors to nursing homes to those people approved by the home. The Health Law Project at the University of Pennsylvania attempted, with interested people from the community, to organize a patients-rights group in a nursing home. The organizers were quickly barred from the home. A federal court issued a temporary restraining order guaranteeing the right of patients, community organizers, and lawyers to meet with each other in the home, but there has been no further judicial development of the right of nursing home patients and lawyers and organizers from the outside to meet together in nursing homes.

5. *Access to information.* The right to information is crucial to serious reform. Total institutions typically protect themselves from scrutiny and criticism by strictly controlling information and limiting public knowledge to their own self-serving press releases. A broad right to information about the operation, ownership, and financing of nursing homes and the degree to which they are in compliance with legal requirements is necessary for patients and their representa-

tives to hold institutions accountable. Nursing homes should also be required to print and distribute, in appropriate languages, a Bill of Rights for residents. Rights are never enforceable unless people know about them.

6. *Due process.* The mortality rate for elderly people transferred from one institution to another is very high. It is sufficiently well documented to have received a name: transfer trauma. The likelihood of transfer trauma can be reduced by involving the elderly person in the transfer decision, allowing him the right to contest it, and familiarizing him, in advance of any move, with the range of alternatives and the characteristics of the new environment.

Individuals are commonly transferred from one nursing home to another in two situations: when a home is closed for noncompliance with legal standards, or when a review committee determines that the individual no longer needs the care provided. In either situation, the individual ought to be entitled, but is now not, to a prior hearing to obtain and provide information and to express his opinion.

The foregoing list, sketchy though it is, describes an institution whose residents are still virtually barren of rights. Most other caring institutions, subjected to sustained litigation during the past decade, are today substantially more limited, at least theoretically, in the discretion they are permitted to exercise. Yet even in those institutions, large areas of discretion continue to exist and to encroach upon the rights of the dependent. Though the general principle that the Bill of Rights should apply to caring institutions is no longer in jeopardy, that principle still needs to be substantially extended. And where it has been established, it needs to be enforced.

Second Principle: Enforcement of constitutional limits is not self-executing and therefore requires an external force.

The capacity of bureaucratic institutions to absorb criticism and even court orders without changing is almost inexhaustible. Though examples are numerous, two should suffice. In 1969, advocates for student rights succeeded in establishing significant legal limits upon the discretion of public school principals in New York City to suspend students unfairly. At the same time, those limits seemed to entitle students to unprecedented due process rights, and were rightly described as a model for the nation. In the year when those legal limits were first imposed, there were approximately thirteen thousand annual suspensions by principals. Eight years later, there were twice that many. Most suspensions violated the Board of Education's own bylaws and were clearly illegal; most were below the high school level; most were part of the pattern of illegal exclusion that had resulted for years in a massive push-out problem reflected in low rates of academic diplomas.

In 1977, the United States Department of Health, Education and Welfare, after an intensive investigation, issued a lengthy report charging the New York City school system with gross illegal discrimination against nonwhite students, especially with respect to suspensions. Such charges were not new. Six years earlier, a civic group deeply involved in the effort to establish student rights had issued a report covering the first year following the enactment of the new legal limits, to see if they were making suspensions fairer. The report concluded they were not. In fact, it was unable to find even a single suspension of the more than a hundred studied where the new rules had been fully observed. *Every* case revealed a violation of rights. A New York *Times* editorial, commenting on the report, characterized it as "a serious indictment" and concluded that "students' rights in many cases appear to have been given short shrift." The editorial concluded:

> Causes for suspension, as cited by the study, range from the ridiculous to the outrageous. To suspend a student for irregular attendance seems like prescribing liquor for an alcoholic. . . . In many cases, principals are charged with having exceeded their authority to suspend as defined by the system's own directives. City educators, who are rightly alarmed by a growing trend of student lawlessness and contempt for authority, should be particularly alert to the damage done to respect for law and justice by official example.*

But neither the editorial nor the civic group's report prodded the Board of Education to enforce the law upon its own employees. Principals continued to refuse to comply and persistently exceeded the new legal limits imposed upon their traditional discretion. One principal even complained that students were being incited to exercise their rights. The official lawlessness of the principals was augmented by the official inaction of the Board of Education. A year later, the same civic group issued an even more extensive report, with similar conclusions. Still, there was no enforcement. Five years later, the number of suspensions had doubled, and the Department of Health, Education and Welfare was threatening to cut off federal funds.

The extended litigation to establish rights for men-

*The New York Times, 20 February, 1971.

tally retarded children at Willowbrook, a state institution on Staten Island, New York, provides another
anguished example. In March 1972, Willowbrook had
a population of 5,200, which was 65 percent over capacity. Children and adults lived packed together in
wards of fifty or more, with little supervision and no
professional staff. One lawyer involved in the case
briefly described the conditions at Willowbrook:

> The wards were large, barren day rooms, rarely con-
> taining even enough chairs for all of the residents. It
> was not unusual to find feces and urine smeared on the
> walls and floor. Residents were either partially clothed
> or naked. It was unusual to find a resident who wasn't
> physically scarred as a result of accidents or abuse.*

On March 17, 1972, several public-interest law groups
sued in federal court in an effort to remedy what one
expert called a "major tragedy." Massive testimony
was given to prove inadequacies of management,
staffing, and budgeting. One witness testified to the
inedible quality and insufficient quantity of food. Another found that most accidents and injuries to residents occurred when they were awakened by staff.
Horror stories flowed into the trial transcript: deaths
by choking that could have been prevented with
proper equipment and adequate staffing; a resident
with a broken leg in a cast infested with bugs and
maggots; another resident with an untended infection
in his eye which, when cleaned, was found to have a
thumbtack imbedded in it. And then there was the
routine use of cattle prods on residents, which the

*Christopher A. Hansen, "Willowbrook," in *Mental Retardation and
Developmental Disabilities: An Annual Review,* edited by Joseph Wortis,
Brunner/Mazel, 1977.

good people at Willowbrook called aversion therapy.

The lawsuit to end these conditions was vigorously resisted by New York State for over three years. Finally, on April 30, 1975, a consent decree was signed by the judge. It ordered extensive relief, requiring immensely detailed changes in staffing, programming, and environment, all to take place within thirteen months. It assured adequate staff/patient ratios, guaranteed standards of privacy, dignity, comfort, and sanitation, reduced the overcrowded population and the maximum number of people permitted in each unit, and set up a review panel of experts to monitor compliance. The incredible amount of time and money spent since 1972 seemed at last to have produced fundamental change.

Yet, two years later, lawyers were back in court seeking contempt citations against state officials for refusal to comply with the court order. Some changes have occurred, but as one lawyer put it, "life has not changed significantly for most of the 5,200 plaintiffs." Why? According to the lawyers, progress has not been impeded by a lack of money, a lack of knowledge, or a lack of administrative capacity. Progress has been impeded by a lack of will, and nothing short of continued efforts to have state officials held in contempt of court seems capable of producing change. And even if conditions at Willowbrook do eventually approach the legal standards contemplated by the court order, there are hundreds of other Willowbrooks to which those standards need to be applied. Test cases are not enough.

What is clear beyond doubt is that the mere declaration of a legal principle by a court means little without more. Lawyers' victories do not imply clients' victories. The last decade can probably be accurately characterized as the beginning of the legal effort to establish rights for the socially dependent. As that effort moves toward completion, a new one must begin, no less inventive and likely to be even more difficult and to meet with even more resistance, to enforce those rights that have been won.

Richard Cloward and Frances Fox Piven have suggested, in another context, that individual social workers should regard themselves as their clients' advocates against the service institutions and thus create of themselves an internal mechanism to enforce and protect the rights of the dependent.* Though that is a commendable suggestion, it is probably insufficient, as Cloward and Piven would be themselves the first to recognize. Most social workers will not take the very real risks inherent in challenging their employers in behalf of their clients. Many of those who do are fired, and *their* legal rights to protect themselves from such firings are far from sufficient. Many social workers thus find themselves faced with a choice between defending their client and sacrificing themselves or saving themselves and becoming accomplices to the abuse of their client. One would hope that individual social workers would make the courageous choice, and fight to restrict the institution's power to violate their rights and those of their clients. Some have. But to expect such a radical choice to be made by many would be illusory.

The more likely remedy is to create strong external adversaries. Such adversaries must be independent of the institution, and beyond its reach, both politically and financially.

Where will such external adversaries come from? In

*Introduction, *Radical Social Work,* Pantheon, 1976.

part, they already exist. To a large extent, the rights movements of the sixties and seventies were enabled and supported by private, voluntary organizations like the American Civil Liberties Union, whose funds came entirely, or predominantly, from private sources. Beyond the reach of political pressure from government agencies under attack, such organizations proved to be an effective and unrelenting external force, at least within the limits of their resources.

Government-funded adversaries proved temporarily effective in many instances, but more often than not were vulnerable to political pressure and emasculated by rules limiting their intervention or by sharp reductions in funds. Other kinds of government aid often proved crucial, however. In several instances —notably including the Willowbrook case—the *federal* government intervened on the side of the dependents and their lawyers against *state* governments. Where the adversary was the state, the federal government was more than sufficiently external to be an effective and powerful adversary.

In response to the very limited resources of even the largest private organizations, federal courts also began to award sizable attorneys' fees, as well as litigation costs, to attorneys representing various dependent groups free of charge. Several courts began explicitly to develop a theory that, by representing individuals in pursuit of their constitutional rights, such "public interest" lawyers were acting as private attorneys-general, and performing a function that was crucial to the implementation of constitutional rights, and therefore worthy of public support through the award of fees for service.

Normally assessed against a defendant government agency, such awards for a while promised to be a significant means of funding external independent adversaries functioning in behalf of people seeking to vindicate their constitutional rights. This promise was abruptly shattered when the Nixon-dominated Supreme Court ruled, in the early seventies, that such awards were not required by the Constitution, and could not be made by federal courts without specific and explicit congressional authorization. Not long after that, and following a substantial lobbying effort by various public-interest groups, Congress did enact an amendment to the Civil Rights Act authorizing federal courts to award attorneys' fees to the winning side in civil rights cases. That statute has been liberally interpreted by the Supreme Court, and substantial awards have been made. Private groups that regularly represent dependent people have certainly begun to rely upon such awards as part of their normal and expected income.

What is clear beyond any doubt is that strong, independent external adversaries are required if individual rights are to be established and enforced against service institutions. Those who are dependent upon the institution must have easy access to such adversaries, who often will be lawyers but who do not need to be lawyers. During the rights movements of the sixties and seventies, such external adversaries often proved to be a critical element in the effort to persist against recalcitrant institutions. Several examples should suffice.

In the early 1960s, at the beginning of the welfare rights movement, independently funded social workers who saw themselves as advocates for their clients against local departments of welfare were able to modify substantially government discretion and were instrumental in making significant gains for welfare recipients. Their accomplishments were a direct result of their independence—*and lasted only as long as their independence was maintained.*

Later in the decade, lay advocates accompanying children and their parents to school-suspension hearings were able to impose major limits on official discretion and were a key element in the struggle to secure student rights. Those advocates were successful only because they were independent of the school, were usually funded and otherwise supported by private organizations, and remained beyond the reach of official reprisals.

At about the same time, vast networks of draft counselors arose spontaneously as a response to the war in Vietnam and the resistance to conscription that it spawned. Most of those draft counselors were not lawyers, though many were backed by lawyers. Supported, employed, and trained by outside civic groups, they collectively enabled tens of thousands of young men to exercise and expand their legal rights against the Selective Service System. Before they were available, hardly anyone ever won a dispute with the Selective Service System. By the early 1970s, in places where draft counseling had reached its peak, 90 percent or more of such disputes ended in victory for the individual.

The effectiveness of such lay advocates was greatly enhanced by the availability of lawyers ready to litigate when less drastic methods did not suffice. Outside organizations began to provide lawyers to challenge in court the discretion of institutions when lay advocates were not able to do so through negotiations or administrative proceedings. Lay advocates began to work closely with lawyers and legal organizations. During those years, most service institutions were literally assaulted by advocacy. Traditional rights were systematically introduced into untraditional settings.

Institutional officials did not react kindly to external adversaries. Bureaucratic discretion was a flower that flourished in obscurity and withered under the light of fair procedures and substantive limitations. Most service professionals resisted the new adversary system and struggled bitterly to keep the light out. They claimed that the adversary system was no part of caring institutions and that its introduction was an obstacle to service.

In reality, the new advocates did not introduce the adversary system to caring institutions. School-suspension hearings had always been adversarial—*from the point of view of the student.* Mental commitment procedures had always been adversarial—*to the unwilling patient.* People evicted from public housing or cut off from welfare always knew who their institutional adversaries were. Children plucked from their parents and moved like old furniture from one foster placement to another always knew that their interests were different from those of their "benefactors."

Orwellian euphemisms accompanied all institutional procedures: searches were called "home visits," dossiers were called "anecdotal records," incarceration was called "placement," and punishment was called "rehabilitation." Children *pushed* out of school were said to have *dropped* out, and school suspensions took place not at hearings but at "guidance conferences" where there were, presumably, no conflicts of interest, but where instead everyone had the same interest—the child's. However polite and gentle such "guidance conferences" may have been at the start, their adversarial nature became clear enough at the end, when the principal or other school official made the decision to suspend. At that moment, fangs were bared and students and their parents stood naked and powerless. At that moment, the "guidance conference" became visible as the adversary proceeding it had always been.

In fact, the new advocates only made the existing adversary system *explicit,* by exposing conflicts of interest between institutions and their clients and by challenging those conflicts openly and directly. The new advocates made the adversary system *fairer* by evening the odds, and that is why they were resisted. They were a countervailing power and they were fought by the managers of service institutions for approximately the same reasons that labor unions were fought by the managers of industry. They were also necessary for the same reasons that labor unions were necessary: no one accustomed to unlimited discretion will willingly give it up. General Motors didn't, and neither did the social institutions of caring.* Therefore, external adversaries were necessary, and remain necessary, both to win and to enforce the rights of dependents.

Third Principle: Every program designed to help the dependent ought to be evaluated, not on the basis of the good it might do, but rather on the basis of the

*Ironically, some labor unions joined their managerial adversaries in a kind of Hitler-Stalin pact against their clients. In many schools, for example, teachers' unions, which had so recently won their own fight to limit managerial discretion, often joined forces with principals and boards of education to resist similar demands by students. Teachers who had justly disrupted entire school systems by strikes in order to force contracts upon school officials that limited managerial powers and thereby secured teachers' rights, now linked arms with their former adversaries and accused students who sought the same rights of disrupting the school. Those who managed the schools and those who worked there thus came to find a common cause in oppressing those whom the schools were designed to serve.

harm it might do. Those programs ought to be adopted that seem to be the least likely to make things worse.

Limits upon the powers of service institutions define individual rights by making certain powers illegitimate. But even when they exercise legitimate powers in behalf of dependent people, service institutions can do—and have done—great harm to those they seek to help. The principle of least harm, though less ambitious, offers a better guideline for legitimate social programs. Though a complete analytical description of the impact that this principle would have on the full range of social services is clearly beyond the scope of this small essay, it would perhaps be useful to examine one group of dependent people—children— in some detail, and describe how the principle of least harm might alter current social programs designed to benefit them.

In some respects, programs for dependent children provide the best vehicle for the illustration of this principle, for in such programs the state acts directly as a surrogate parent. In commenting on the stance we should take when we intervene, Anna Freud, Albert J. Solnit, and Joseph Goldstein have recently applied our third principle directly to programs for children:

> In the long run, the child's chances will be better if the law is less pretentious and ambitious in its aim, that is, if it confines itself to the avoidance of harm.*

When the state intervenes, they go on to say, it ought always to choose "the least detrimental available alternative for safeguarding the child's growth and development."

*Beyond the Best Interests of the Child, Free Press, 1973.

The history of public intervention in the lives of children is littered with programs that came clothed in the garb of reform, but that later were revealed to have resulted in substantial, though perhaps unintended, harm. No better example exists of this unhappy phenomenon than the effort, by 1977 almost a century old, to remove troubled children from their homes and seal them off in an environment sheltered from the harsh world and enriched with programs that promised to heal their souls. In New York, such children were called PINS—Persons in Need of Supervision. In other states, they were called CHINS—Children in Need of Supervision. We never lacked for acronyms.

Originally the product of nineteenth-century liberal reform, the institutionalization of children for the ostensibly benevolent purpose of rehabilitation too often was revealed in fact as an Orwellian nightmare of custody, confinement, and punishment. Words like "training school" were substituted for "prison," "child-care worker" for "guard," "campus" for "prison grounds," and "cottage" for "cell block." The language of deception did its work well: it didn't sound so bad when we spoke of children sent to live in cottages on a campus where they would be helped by child-care workers. It sounded worse when we spoke the truth: too often children were sentenced to cells in prisons under the custody of guards.

Some "training schools" made liberal use of solitary confinement. They called it "the quiet room." Until protracted litigation struck it down in New York, for example, solitary confinement was a fairly common practice. During one three-month period during the early 1970s, in only two of New York's twelve training schools, 130 children were kept in solitary confinement for a total of 542 days. These children were not just sent to their rooms: we are talking about conditions that compared with those faced by the Count of Monte Cristo: a five-by-eight-foot airless cell, smelling of urine, with bare walls, no furniture, a single light bulb, and a closed, barred window. One child was left there for weeks, in pajamas, allowed nothing to read, taken out only at appointed times to the toilet, and given food on a tray. She slept on an eighteen-inch board that protruded from the wall. Affidavits from several of these children showed that sometimes they became so desperate they swallowed open safety pins in order to be taken to the infirmary.

There was incredible resistance to any change in these practices. New York State resisted for more than a year litigation challenging such solitary confinement. In 1970 the state legislature passed a moderate bill limiting solitary confinement of children in state training schools. Former Governor Nelson Rockefeller vetoed even that limited bill. Why? Because the state Department of Social Services told him that such practices were required to maintain discipline, and discipline was part of the program for helping needy children. Most of these children were not juvenile delinquents; none of them had committed a crime. They were there because they had been victims of neglect or parental abuse, or because poverty and its attendant problems had ground their families into dust. And the state helped out by putting them in the hole.

The traditional answer of the reformers to such sorry conditions has been to defend the idea of benevolent institutionalization, cite their lofty goals, and advocate the improvement of the institution. "Do not throw out the baby with the bathwater," they counseled. "Get rid of solitary confinement, but continue to permit us the discretion to institutionalize children for their own good." But the capacity of the institution to absorb defeat and continue to violate the rights of those it claimed to help proved nearly inexhaustible. Several years after a federal judge had limited the length of solitary confinement to no more than twenty-four consecutive hours, two employees of a state training school emerged to reveal that the school had invented the practice of confinement for twenty-three hours, release for one hour, and confinement for another twenty-three hours in order to avoid the court's restrictions. The response of reformers—their hope that institutionalization could be made humane —proved destructive to those they sought to help. If they had focused not on the good they had hoped to do but rather on the harm they were likely to do, they might have avoided destroying a lot of children.

The distinction is important. We have operated in the past on the theory of incarceration for the good of the inmate. Since we were trying to *improve* the inmate, since we were trying to *rehabilitate* him, since everything we did to him was supposedly *not punitive* but rather *in his own best interests*, it followed that we could do anything we believed would work. The limits on our power were effectively removed by the benevolence of our goals. If instead we were barred from doing anything that was likely to *debilitate* the inmate, we would have to proceed within much narrower limits, and with much less restrictive means. The likelihood of harm to the objects of our good intentions would be much less.

Under our present system, the likelihood of harm is immense. Several hundred thousand children, mostly early adolescents, are subjected to PINS arrests annually throughout the United States. About

60 percent of these end up in the custody of the state, and about half of those confined spend some time in "severe detention." Children arrested as PINS are more likely to end up in the custody of the state than children arrested as juvenile delinquents, even though PINS children have committed no act that would constitute a crime if committed by an adult.

What exactly did these children do? Why were they placed in the custody of the state? Recent statistics show that the chief reason is "truancy," followed closely by "running away from home." Other leading reasons were "staying out late," "undesirable companions," and "sexual acting-out."

There are two other characteristics that most of these children share: they are poor and they are not white. That the PINS statute lends itself to particularly harsh enforcement against racial minorities and the poor, while immunizing middle-class children who engage in identical behavior, has been the subject of much comment.* Indeed, an officially authorized New York study has documented the fact that black and Puerto Rican children are relegated to Family Court for usually punitive and always coercive treatment, while white and middle-class children are served by noncoercive community agencies.** Middle-class chil-

*See Nondelinquent Children in New York: The Need for Alternatives to Institutional Treatment, 8 Colum. J. Law & Soc. Prob. 251 (1972); President's Commission on Law Enforcement and Administration of Justice, Task Force Report: Juvenile Delinquency and Youth Crime (1967); Wolfgang, The Culture of Youth; Werthman, The Function of Social Definitions in the Development of Delinquent Careers; and Berg, Economic Factors in Delinquency.

**Committee on Mental Health Services Inside and Outside the Family Court in the City of New York, Juvenile Justice Confounded: Pretensions and Realities of Treatment Services (1972), pp. 21–32.

dren who "refuse to obey," who "associate with undesirable companions," who "run away from home," do
not normally find their way to Family Court as PINS.
They are sent to boarding school or military acade-
mies, to private psychologists and group therapy. In
order to escape the summer heat they go to camp—
unlike poor children who resort to the streets and
thereby incur PINS adjudications predicated on
"keeping late hours." Sexual precocity, too, is more
visible where poverty demands too much communal
living.

What the families of poor children lack, above all, is
money. With sufficient wealth, they could hire governesses if the mother was neglectful, or psychiatrists if
the child was troubled, or tutors or homemakers or
baby-sitters. But the families of the poor cannot afford
such services, and so the state helps out by incarcerat-
ing their children. It costs more than $20,000 a year to
maintain one child in a state training school. This pays
the salaries of his guards, and maintains the cells and
buildings and walls and fences. In less restrictive, but
still coercive, settings, it can cost the state close to
$10,000 a year per child. Thus a family of three PINS
children, separated from each other as well as their
parents, can cost the state at least $30,000 to $60,000
a year. Think of what that money could provide in
services that went directly to the family—private
school tuitions, special tutors, psychiatric help, everything a family with money could buy. But the state will
not spend such a sum on the children of the poor; it
would rather pay other people to lock them up.

Any arguments in favor of continuing PINS jurisdiction, and the coercive power to imprison children,
must rest on the results achieved. In particular, according to the principle suggested here of measuring

programs not by the good we hope they will accomplish but by the harm they are likely to do, what has resulted from early court intervention in children's lives? Is it true that such intervention saves children, as all the bright reformers promised, or are children made worse? Is it true that early court intervention prevents later criminal behavior, or is later criminal behavior more likely?

The evidence is that early court intervention does not save children, but rather makes them worse. Studies in the 1930s and 1940s by psychologists and sociologists such as Sheldon and Eleanor Glueck, Clifford Shaw, and Henry D. McKay demonstrated very high rates of subsequent arrest for real crimes of children who had spent time in training schools. Later studies have confirmed these findings.

Summarizing the available research for the President's Commission on Law Enforcement and Administration of Justice,* sociologist Edwin Lemert pointed out that youth who come under court jurisdiction commit more rather than fewer crimes later on. "The conclusion that the court processing rather than the behavior in some way helps to fix and perpetuate delinquency in many cases is hard to escape," Lemert says.

Yet there are some who would defend early court intervention by trying to argue that the reason children under court jurisdiction commit more crimes later on than other children is that they are bad to begin with. That is why they come under court jurisdiction in the first place, the argument goes. This argument, though appealing at first glance, has been put

---

*Task Force Report, *Juvenile Delinquency and Youth Crime*, Appendix D.

to rest by a remarkable study by three prominent sociologists and criminologists.* Norval Morris, professor of law at the University of Chicago Law School and author of *The Future of Imprisonment,* calls the Philadelphia study "a rare turning point in criminological research." Certainly it presents the only hard statistics I have seen about what actually happens to children who pass through our juvenile courts. The research traced the lives of all ten thousand boys born in 1945, who lived in Philadelphia between their tenth and eighteenth birthdays.

Thirty-five percent of the boys had a police record at some time between the ages of ten and eighteen, and these were divided into groups of single offenders, multiple offenders, chronic offenders, and then again into socioeconomic and racial groups. They were also divided according to what happened to them: some boys were handled "informally" outside court jurisdiction; some were arrested and had the charges dismissed; some were punished by receiving sentences of probation or incarceration.

Among the sadly predictable findings: blacks are treated more harshly than whites, are more likely to be formally arrested, less likely to have their cases informally settled, and more likely to receive a court penalty such as probation or incarceration. After examining all the variables that might legitimately account for this racial disparity, the authors conclude that the different treatment was based primarily on race, *not on other factors such as recidivism or the seriousness of the crime.*

Another grim finding: the more punitive the treat-

Delinquency in a Birth Cohort, Marvin E. Wolfgang, Robert M. Figlio, and Thorsten Sellin, University of Chicago Press, 1972.

ment (institutionalization, fine, or probation) a young-
ster receives, the more likely he is to commit more
serious crimes with greater rapidity than those who
are less constrained by the judicial and correctional
systems. "We must conclude," say the authors, "that
the juvenile justice system, at its best, has no effect on
the subsequent behavior of adolescent boys and, at its
worst, has a deleterious effect on future behavior."
Thus, not only is coercive court intervention a waste
of money, but it seems to do little more than create a
class of future criminals.

The consequences indicated by this study are stun-
ning. If children receive punitive treatment by the
courts not according to the seriousness of their offense
but rather according to race; and if children who receive punitive treatment are not helped, but on the
contrary are more likely to commit crimes later on,
then what are we doing? The answer is inescapable:
we are destroying those whom we would help, and we
are creating criminals for the future.

There has been much clamor recently about cod-
dling young criminals. Many people are advocating
longer sentences for young people who commit vio-
lent crimes. Perhaps such longer sentences are justified, if only to protect society. But if serious crimes
ought to be dealt with by more imprisonment, then
nonserious misbehavior, which does not constitute a
crime, ought to be dealt with by means other than
imprisonment or the threat of imprisonment. And
consider the numbers involved: of the approximately
one million children under sixteen who are arrested
annually, about five hundred are arrested for murder.
But nearly 200,000 are incarcerated for noncrimes
such as breaking curfew, or running away. Perhaps we
have to lock up the five hundred. But why lock up the

200,000, especially when the evidence shows that locking them up increases the likelihood of later criminal behavior? The principle of least harm would prohibit coercive jurisdiction over noncriminal juvenile behavior and limit state intervention to less drastic approaches.

Perhaps such less drastic approaches would not do much good. Perhaps the provision of homemakers or governesses or other services on a voluntary basis to families who cannot afford to purchase such services won't help much. Perhaps finding children who run away and returning them to their homes seems futile. Perhaps establishing places where older runaway children—who may be running away for good reason—can go to live seems too indulgent. But at least the likelihood of harm from such approaches seems low. Not even that much can be said about PINS.

Significantly, federal courts are now beginning to recognize the principle of least harm in other, related areas. In the Willowbrook case, Judge Orrin Judd ruled that even though the mentally retarded residents of Willowbrook could legally leave, and even though they had no constitutional right to treatment by the state, they nonetheless were entitled to be protected from harm once the state undertook their care and custody.

Judge Judd's ruling had explosive consequences. Having ruled that residents of Willowbrook were constitutionally entitled to be protected from harm, he then ordered very specific services, which he found were required to enforce that entitlement. These included a prohibition against seclusion; immediate hiring of additional ward attendants sufficient to ensure a ratio of one attendant to nine residents; immediate hiring of eighty-five more nurses, thirty more physical therapists, fifteen more doctors, and sufficient recreation staff; immediate and continuing repair of all inoperable toilets; and other relief.

Nearly two years later, after an extensive trial, his order was substantially expanded. "Protection from harm," ruled Judge Judd, "requires relief more extensive than this court originally contemplated, because harm can result not only from neglect but from conditions which cause regression or which prevent development of an individual's capabilities." Unprecedented levels of services and care were ordered in order to enforce the right to be free from harm. Specific requirements for education, recreation, physical therapy, and speech pathology were set. Specific areas of potential abuse such as restraints, forced labor, behavior modification, research, and medication were limited and regulated. Specific and detailed staff ratios were set. Finally, the population of Willowbrook was ordered reduced, within a specific period of time, from 5,200 residents' when the litigation began to no more than 250. "The primary goal," said the court order, "shall be to ready each resident, with due regard for his or her own disabilities and with full appreciation for his or her own capabilities for development, for life in the community at large." Detailed, comprehensive plans for additional community facilities and programs were ordered developed.

The key point was that the court found large-scale institutionalization itself harmful, quite aside from the Dickensian conditions that prevailed at Willowbrook. (Some said those conditions were an inevitable consequence of large-scale institutionalization.) And it ordered a remedy that was less likely to be harmful. Significantly, that remedy involved a move away from large-scale, centralized facilities and toward the more natural settings of homes and communities, buttressed by local, decentralized services. It was almost as if the court had realized that large, central institutions were, and had always been, antithetical to the natural family and that the biological imperative for love and caring could not exist except in its natural setting, and certainly not in places like Willowbrook. If that was true, then the way to apply the principle of least harm was to fashion the delivery of services in a manner that simulated the family as much as possible. That implied services in the home as well as in the community, and on a decentralized basis. It also implied an end to large, centralized institutions.

At about the same time the Willowbrook case was being decided, other courts also began to articulate the principle of least harm. In Iowa, two parents sued the state for permanently removing their children and terminating their parental rights on the basis of vague and ill-defined standards, such as not providing "necessary parental care and protection" and of being "detrimental to the physical or mental health or morals" of their children. In fact, such standards allowed the state to take the Alsagers' children away permanently, even though they were not abused or in any serious danger, but simply because the state felt that the children would be better off elsewhere. The evidence of "neglect" was skimpy in the extreme. There had been neighbors' reports of unwashed dishes and of the children appearing unkempt while playing in the street, and sometimes arriving late at school, but little else. After years of litigation, during which time several of the children had been in the custody of the state, a federal court in Iowa came close to accepting the principle of least harm:

Termination has thus failed to provide the Alsager children with either stable or improved lives. Based on their parents' capabilities, the Court cannot say that separation has benefited the children in any discernible way. In the eyes of plaintiffs' experts, they have been harmed. One lesson emerges clearly from this sad treatment. Termination is a drastic, final step which, when improvidently employed, can be fraught with danger. Accordingly, to preserve the best interests of both parents and children, the Court deems that termination must only occur where more harm is likely to befall the child by staying with his parents than by being permanently separated from them.*

Interestingly enough, the federal court stopped short of mandating direct services as an alternative to removal. If the state believed the Alsager children needed help, why was it not willing to provide services to the children's parents? The court shied away from "saddling the state with service-oriented responsibilities which its limited resources may not allow." But that, of course, was not the question. It was never a question of resources. The state was all too willing to allocate substantial resources to the children *if they were removed from their parents.* But the state was not willing to provide equivalent services—probably at less cost—directly to the family in its own home. The principle of least harm would have required the state to provide such services, on a voluntary basis, and would have initially barred the removal of the children. Whether and to what extent such services would have helped the children is unclear. What is clear, as the court noted, is that the harm that came to the children when the state plucked them from their family would have been avoided. Since the chil-

Alsager v. *District Court of Polk County,* 518 F.2d 1160 (8th Cir. 1975).

dren were concededly not in danger of being neglected or abused, the state's intervention, if intervention was appropriate at all, should have been guided by the desire to avoid harm. In fact, the state risked harm—and achieved it—in its zeal to do good.

The *Alsager* case raised issues that are endemic to child-care programs of various kinds throughout the country. The case of Joey Miller provides an agonizing illustration. Joey was a black ten-year-old boy living with his mother, but not his father.

Joey's mother was employed as a secretary, but was not finding it easy making ends meet. Joey had been having problems in school, and the school notified his mother that he would be suspended as a result. Both the school psychologist and a private child psychiatrist who examined him recommended that he be placed in a residential treatment program for a brief time. Unable to afford private programs, the mother finally found one school that was willing to accept the boy and be paid by public funds through the Bureau of Child Welfare.

Almost immediately, however, she was told by child welfare officials that her son could not go to that school unless she signed certain required papers. The papers, if signed, would have effectively turned over custody to the state, and would have forced her to concede that she was an inadequate and unfit mother, when in fact she was anything but. When she balked, she was told that her son would not receive help unless she signed, and that if she didn't sign, the city might bring neglect proceedings against her and take the child away. The sole basis for neglect would be her refusal to sign. Privately, some of those officials conceded the monstrosity of the trap that Mrs. Miller and her son were caught in. But publicly, and in court, they resisted her attempt to break free from that trap.

Patterns of public funding were the locks that kept the trap shut against Joey Miller and his mother. Complicated federal and state statutes combined to provide funds for needed services, but only if those who depended upon services waived their rights. Joey could have the state's help if he gave up his mother, and she could help her child if she relinquished him to the state.

The principle of least harm would avoid this dilemma. Removal of the child into state custody would no longer be a permissible condition of needed services. In fact, separating the child from his mother's custody would be viewed as a drastic and harmful step. The avoidance of such a step would become the first priority of our social response. The same services would be provided, but without transferring the child's custody to the state. The benefit of those services to the child would remain speculative, precisely as it is now, but the harm that would likely flow from state custody could be avoided.

This case is important because Joey Miller and his mother are members of a large and growing class of single-parent families. The number and percentage of single-parent families has been increasing steadily in recent decades. In 1960 about 10 percent of New York families with children under eighteen had only one parent living in the household. By 1976 it was almost 30 percent. In most single-parent families—over 95 percent—the mother is the single parent. As a result, very large numbers of children have come to live with their mother only. By 1973 over 30 percent of all New York City children were living with their mother and no father. And though the trend is not so dramatic in the rest of the United States, it is dramatic enough:

one child in six lives with his or her mother only. Many thousands of these children are on welfare, and dependent upon the state, because their mothers cannot work or cannot find work. Many others are left uncared for, or inadequately cared for, during at least part of the day if their mothers do work.* We know that there will be social programs ostensibly designed to help these children. What we don't know are the principles that will shape those programs, or whether they will manage at least to avoid bringing more harm to children already in trouble.

Many of these children will end up in long-term foster care, bouncing from placement to placement, their lives subject at every moment to the grace and whim of the state. There are between 500,000 and 750,000 children now living in foster care throughout the country, and the state's intervention in their lives is not guided by the principle of least harm.

Perhaps the most harmful thing for a growing child is instability, the lack of a permanent family, the absence of the steady love and support of a particular adult. The principle of least harm would seek above all to avoid such instability, yet current public policy seems everywhere to encourage it. The right to services—such as homemakers, tutors, psychological services, etc. (which affluent families in trouble can purchase)—provided directly to the family in its home, as an alternative to the removal of the child into state custody, does not exist. As a result, too many children are removed and inappropriately placed into foster care.

*The foregoing facts concerning children living in single-parent families were drawn from a remarkably informative report entitled *State of the Child: New York City, II*, by Trude Lash, and published by the Foundation for Child Development, June 1980.

Once in long-term foster care, the establishment of permanent, loving relationships is actively discouraged. Meaningful relationships with the biological parents are rare because public officials and foster care agencies do not adequately encourage them and do not provide sufficient services to facilitate an early return of the child. After a certain point, therefore, return to the biological family almost never occurs. Of children in foster care for a year or more, for example, 80 percent of changes in their placement are from one foster placement to another. Moreover, meaningful relationships with foster parents are often frowned upon by foster care agencies because foster care is viewed as a temporary measure, even though the *average* duration of foster care in New York City, for example, was six years as of 1977.

Adoption is also a rarely used device, so new permanent families are rarely established. Of the thousands of children in foster care who have no relationship with their biological parents and who are available for adoption, very few are actually adopted. The cumulative effect of such public policies is to condemn many foster children, and especially black foster children, to an endless limbo that reduces their chances for a normal childhood and sentences them to instability until they are at last released by the passage of time, old enough finally to be discharged, but in all likelihood emotionally damaged beyond repair.

Several studies bear out these conclusions:

1. A study undertaken by the New York State Board of Social Welfare in conjunction with the New School for Social Research, entitled "Foster Care Needs and Alternatives to Placement: A Projection for 1975–1985," found that "many children placed outside their homes could have stayed home, or could have re-

turned home at an earlier time with a better likelihood of remaining there, if appropriate supportive services had been available." (Quoted in Temporary [N.Y.] State Commission on Child Welfare, 1976 Annual Report, The Children of the State, II, pp. 9–10.)

2. In a 1975 report prepared by the State Board of Social Welfare entitled "Foster Care Needs and Alternatives to Placement: A Plan for Action," it was noted that "the lack of funding for community-based preventive and supportive services for families at risk has often led to the inappropriate entry of many children into the foster care system" (p. 3).

3. A survey (January 7, 1977) by the Community Council of Greater New York, entitled "Children, Families and Foster Care: New Insights from Research in New York City," found that in 1975 there were nearly thirty thousand children in foster care in New York City; that the average time a child spends in foster care is 5.4 years; that 20 percent of children now in foster care have been in care for at least ten years; that more than 40 percent of children in foster care were inappropriately placed; that after the first year of placement the chances of a return home dropped sharply; and that one-half the potential adoption case load had not even been freed for adoption. There are recent indications that some of these statistics have worsened since 1977. For example, over 31 percent of foster-care children have been in the custody of the state for more than six years; for children entering foster care as infants, the average duration was over seven years; over half are moved at least twice from one place to another and nearly a third are moved three times or more; and although 64 percent of children studied in one survey should have been freed for adoption, less than 18 percent actually were freed. Finally, it is worth noting that most of these statistics

describe foster care in New York; there are persuasive indications, though few reliable studies, that the situation is much worse throughout the country.

Thus the system of foster care as it actually operates is *not* a system of temporary care; children are removed from their families when they shouldn't be and then rarely are returned to their biological parents and even more rarely are adopted. Most children in foster care for more than a year spend their entire childhoods in transit: of 1,505 children moved from foster care during 1973–74, only 202 were returned home, and only 103 were placed for adoption. The remaining 1,200 were shifted to another foster placement.

The principle of least harm would minimize these destructive results by limiting the initial intervention. Removal of the child from its biological family would become a last resort, the most drastic step possible when no other alternative will suffice. The biological imperative for caring and benevolence would be left intact, insofar as that is possible, by providing supportive services directly to the child and its family on a voluntary basis.

Once a child is removed from the biological family, foster care would be seen as a highly temporary emergency measure, and the child would not be allowed to drift aimlessly toward the age of majority. Contacts between the child and its biological parents would be encouraged, enabled, and maintained as if the child was in a hospital for a brief illness. Priority would be placed on an early return, and services would be provided to facilitate that return and make it permanent.

In those cases where the child has been abandoned or legally surrendered, or when all efforts to keep the family together have failed and the child's ties to its biological family have been irretrievably severed, the creation of a new, permanent, stable home through adoption would be required. Currently, exactly the opposite is true. Services are rarely provided outside foster care, and adoption of long-term foster children almost never occurs. The principle of least harm is nowhere to be found in our child-care systems, any more than it can be found in the systems we have to take care of the elderly, the mentally impaired, or the poor.

In all these systems, the dependent are removed from their homes, from their families, and from their communities. Whatever biological imperative for caring may exist is systematically severed. It is simply not possible to avoid doing harm in places like Willowbrook, in most nursing homes, or in the systems we have today to "help" children in trouble. Institutionalization itself must be avoided. Efforts should be made to help the dependent maintain themselves as normally as possible, in familiar surroundings, and among significant other people. If the dependent need help it should be provided, but on their own terms. To anyone who has stayed in a hospital for even a week and contemplated staying a lifetime, these general goals should be self-evident.

Today, our caring systems are a long way from these goals. Virtually every caring system we have keeps its eye on the good it hopes to accomplish and blinks at the harm it is doing. As a result, hundreds of thousands —perhaps millions—of people are violated every day of their lives by the encroachments of their ostensible benefactors. No matter where the Betty Higdens of this world run, there is an institution close behind them, or just ahead.

In a curious way, the principle of least harm bears a close relationship to the old political dictum: that government is best that governs least. And of course that dictum comes from the time when most people feared the excessive power of government and bridled it with a Bill of Rights. More recently, that dictum has been the battle cry of political conservatives, who seemed always to set themselves against humane public programs. During the middle third of the twentieth century, America, increasingly dominated by political liberals, became more inclined to trust the government. Beginning with the New Deal, political benevolence became institutionalized on a scale never before imaginable. The discretion of government in general, and of the federal executive branch in particular, expanded itself beyond all prior limits. Government became our friend, and we grew insensitive to its potential encroachments.

The pathological result of that development was Richard Nixon. Before he was stopped—barely in the nick of time and largely as a result of several fortuitous accidents—he came to believe that in the name of national security he could do anything. His doctrine of inherent power—the notion that law did not limit the president if the ends sought were sufficiently important—effectively removed the limits imposed by the Bill of Rights and left us all without rights, defenseless against the encroachments of what he considered to be in our best interests.

During the same period of time that the political institutions of government were expanding their discretion, the social institutions of caring were expanding theirs, and with similar results. The reimposition of the Bill of Rights upon the presidency during the 1973–74 impeachment campaign came precisely at the point when the movement to establish limits on the discretion of social institutions also reached its peak. The reemergence of the original understanding politically came after a decade of effort to apply the original understanding socially. The Bill of Rights seemed finally to overcome the imperial presidency precisely when it was struggling to overcome the imperial school principal, the imperial caseworker, and the imperial state psychiatrist.

That we might overreact to Richard Nixon and bridle the presidency too much worries some observers. In similar fashion, there are those social critics who worry that the rights movement will impose too many limits on the social institutions of caring and encourage the neglect of the dependent. Both worries have some merit, since every reform has its own unintended effects. Few—and least of all political liberals —would wish to return to a time when social programs did not exist and the dependents were left to their own agonies, just as few would wish to return to the eighteenth-century version of the presidency. But it is doubtful that we need to worry too much about the powers of government. We have only recently, and incompletely, leavened our trust in government with that fear of its excesses that informed the early Americans. As they knew, and we must constantly remind ourselves, power tends to expand itself voraciously; it is liberty that is fragile and always in danger of destruction. In adopting the Bill of Rights, the early Americans hardly rejected the idea of governmental power sufficient to achieve legitimate social ends. The proposed constitution was intended to grant substantial powers to the federal government, and it did. The Bill of Rights was added not to negate those powers but to limit them, not to paralyze the government's ability to meet social needs but rather to guarantee against government excesses. The notion of rights never implied governmental neglect—neither in the eighteenth century or today. Rights merely implied certain limits to the methods government could employ in pursuit of legitimate social ends. It was only during the aberrational time of the Progressives that rights came to be seen as inconsistent with needs, and it is the residue of that view which we confront today.

The three principles set forth in this essay seek only to restore that balance between individual rights and social needs that was part of the original understanding. No one ever suggested that the Constitution was an instrument of governmental neglect. Indeed, our history describes a steady expansion of government powers and social programs, often at the expense of individual rights. Therefore, the three principles set forth here cannot reasonably be opposed on the ground that they might breed neglect. Certainly, they leave ample room for government power to fulfill its ostensible obligations. What they do not permit is the excessive zeal that often accompanies government power, whether well-intentioned or not. What they provide is minimal protection for individual rights. Therefore, these three principles deserve to be repeated everywhere, and written into all social legislation.

One pauses, of course, at the prospect of such repetition. How many times do we have to listen to the Bill of Rights refrain? Well, as André Gide told us, "Everything that needs to be said has already been said. But since no one was listening, everything must be said again." And so once more: the midnight knock at the door is always inherent in governmental power. In one century, it comes in the form of a British soldier; in another, a caseworker. The encroachment of power upon liberty has many disguises.

FURTHER READING

Annas, George J. *The Rights of Hospital Patients.* ACLU Handbook Series. New York: Avon, 1975.

Bailyn, Bernard. *Ideological Origins of the American Revolution.* Cambridge, Mass.: Belknap Press, 1967.

Bailyn, Bernard, and Garrett, J. N., eds. *Pamphlets of the American Revolution, 1750–1776.* Cambridge, Mass.: Harvard University Press, 1965.

Brant, Irving. *The Bill of Rights.* Indianapolis, Ind.: Bobbs-Merrill, 1965.

Children's Defense Fund. *Children Out of School in America.* Washington, D. C.: Children's Defense Fund, 1974.

Cloward, Richard, and Piven, Frances Fox. Forward to *Radical Social Work,* Roy Bailey and Mike Brake, eds. New York: Pantheon Books, 1976.

————. *Regulating the Poor.* New York: Pantheon Books, 1971.

Dorsen, Norman, ed. *The Rights of Americans.* New York: Pantheon Books, 1971.

Dorsen, Norman; Bender, Paul; and Neuborne, Burt, eds. *Political and Civil Rights in the United States* 4th ed. Boston: Little, Brown, 1976.

Douglas, William D. *An Almanac of Liberty.* Westport, Conn.: Greenwood Press, 1973.

Ennis, Bruce. *Prisoners of Psychiatry.* New York: Harcourt, Brace, Jovanovich, 1972.

Ennis, Bruce and Siegel, Loren. *The Rights of Mental Patients.* ACLU Handbook Series. New York: Avon, 1973.

Friedman, Paul. *The Rights of the Mentally Retarded.* ACLU Handbook Series. New York: Avon, 1977.

Goffman, Erving. *Asylums.* New York: Doubleday, 1961.

Goldstein, Joseph. *Beyond the Best Interests of the Child.* New York: Free Press, 1973.

Kittrie, Nicholas M. *The Right to Be Different.* Baltimore: The Johns Hopkins Press, 1971.

Lash, Trude. *The State of the Child.* New York: Foundations for Child Development, 1976.

Law, Sylvia and Neuborne, Burt. *The Rights of the Poor.* ACLU Handbook Series. New York: Avon, 1974.

Levine, Alan and Cary, Eve. *The Rights of Students.* ACLU Handbook Series. New York: Avon, 1973.

Levy, Leonard W. *Jefferson and Civil Liberties: The Darker Side* rev. ed. New York: Quadrangle, 1973.

Mill, John Stuart. *On Liberty.* New York: W. W. Norton, 1975.

Norwick, Kenneth P., ed. *Your Legal Rights* rev. ed. New York: The John Day Co., 1975.

Piven, Frances Fox. and Cloward, Richard A. *Poor People's Movements.* New York: Pantheon Books, 1977.

Platt, Anthony. *The Child Savers.* Chicago: University of Chicago Press, 1969.

Rothman, David. *The Discovery of the Asylum.* Boston: Little, Brown, 1971.

Sussman, Alan. *The Rights of Children.* ACLU Handbook Series. New York: Avon, 1976.

Wolfgang, Marvin, et al. *Delinquency in a Birth Cohort.* Chicago: University of Chicago Press, 1972.

AFTERWORD

From the summer of 1977 (when the authors of *Doing Good* made their last revisions) until the fall of 1980 (when I was asked to write this afterword), many of the ideas and policies analyzed in these essays have become increasingly familiar, acceptable, and standard practice in American society. One would be hard-pressed today to find willing defenders of the notion that high school principals should be allowed summarily to expel students whose dress or length of hair offends their taste, or that prison wardens should be allowed summarily to commit inmates to dark and dank solitary cells for weeks on end. It now seems only fair that welfare recipients, mental patients, and juveniles not be left completely vulnerable to the benevolence of social workers, psychiatrists, and judges—an attitude that was hardly prevalent only a few decades ago. In all, the new rights movement has established a floor under the liberties of minorities, no small achievement given the strength and appeal of the Progressive ideology.

That said, it is no less apparent or significant that the next steps in the rights movement, the second-stage questions about the limits on benevolence and paternalism, are becoming acutely controversial and divisive. In the mid-1970s it was not only the rights litigators but a substantial number of professionals who came to believe (some eagerly, others more reluctantly) that the record of abuses and failures in the exercise of discretion was disappointing enough to justify a swing back of the pendulum; some checks on doing good were appropriate. Yet, with greater speed than one might have anticipated, this consensus is splintering, with each side faulting the other for breaking faith. From the perspective of professionals and administrators, civil libertarian lawyers have become so enamored of establishing rights that they completely forget the significance of anything else, whether it is patients' need for treatment or society's need for self-protection. The civil libertarians, on their side, are persuaded that professionals cannot entertain any self-doubt when it comes to the wisdom of their own paternalism or surrender any measure of discretion. In this atmosphere, the next steps that might be taken to promote a liberty model are subject to intense dispute.

The debates have been especially acrimonious where the professionals' credentials are the most substantial, where the rights movement has confronted the discretion of doctors and psychiatrists. The prospect that the two sides might join together to satisfy clients' rights and needs, to see to it that the objects of benevolence were allowed to exercise choice without losing the benefits of expert assistance, has not materialized. What has emerged instead is open and declared warfare.

One critical case in point is the deinstitutionalization of the mentally disabled. In the 1970s this policy was not only very prominent on the litigators' agenda but also received encouragement and support from many individual psychiatrists and their professional organizations, from the established American Psychiatric Association to the more radical American Orthopsychiatric Association. All parties seemed to agree that the abuse and neglect at such facilities as Partlow (Alabama's state institution for the retarded) or Bryce (Alabama's state institution for the mentally ill) or Willowbrook (New York's institution for the retarded) were so gross that the prospect of a federal court ordering a reduction in overcrowding (via a right to live in "the least restrictive alternative") and an improvement in services (via a "right to treatment" or "protection from harm") was highly desirable. Indeed, a number of fiscal conservatives joined—and strengthened—the coalition, believing that deinstitutionalization would be so economical that states would be able to reduce public mental-health expenditures.

It did not take very long, however, for the alliance to come apart and a backlash to set in. Professionals began testifying against deinstitutionalization, many of their organizations were no longer willing to join in lawsuits as amici, and right-wing groups led protests against community care. In the fall of 1978, for example, several well-known and reputable psychiatrists and psychologists testified before Judge Frank Johnson in Alabama that a substantial number of Partlow's residents ought not to leave the facility. They were so deeply retarded that treatment would constitute cruel and unusual punishment; what they required was custodial care within an institution. In this spirit, a federal court decision to remove clients from Pennsylvania's institution for the retarded and place them in the community (as originally ordered in the *Pennhurst* case) was appealed all the way to the Supreme Court (where it is now pending), and at each step, professionals gave depositions arguing that deinstitutionalization had moved too fast and too far. Residents had needs that only institutions could serve; attorneys did not speak for their clients. It was far better to trust to the experts to decide on placement, and federal courts should get out of the business of telling doctors what to do.

The antagonism between psychiatrists and libertarian attorneys was even sharper on the question of patients' right to refuse treatment. Boston Federal Judge Joseph Tauro recently ruled that residents in institutions had the right to accept or refuse medication. Some emergency exceptions aside, patients had a constitutional guarantee of privacy against "powerful and potentially mind-altering drugs." The victory was very much in keeping with the agenda of the rights movement; what was more unusual was the bitterness of the psychiatrists' attack on the court opinion. Two young practitioners characterized it as establishing patients' "right to rot," and Alan Stone, a president of the American Psychiatric Association, found another example to illustrate his claim that attorneys "have treated rights as if they constituted the needs of the mentally ill."

The counterreaction to the rights movement has been fierce not only from experts and professionals but from still more traditional sources of authority: parents and defenders of the family. Here disputes focus on children's rights. It was one thing to bring some procedural protections into juvenile court proceedings, to reduce the arbitrariness of school disciplinary procedures, and to give greater consideration to the well-being of children in resolving custody battles in divorce cases. But it is quite another to alter the balance of authority within the family between parent and child. The father in a recent *New Yorker* cartoon who asks his child at the dinner table, "Do you mean if I make you drink your milk, you'll sue me?" seemingly ought not to receive a "yes" answer. In other words, when children's rights move from the courtroom and classroom into the home, the issue becomes much more complicated and controversial.

As is not uncommon when questions of rights become so divisive, a case that posed the central questions recently came before the Supreme Court. Both the facts in *Parham v. J.L. and J.R.* and the Court's decision (June 29, 1979) clarify why children's rights is so disputed an issue. To those who are uneasy with a rights orientation, the decision is a statement of self-evident principles. To advocates of children's rights, *Parham* ranks with *Dred Scott* in violating the basic rights of a minority.

Parham involved J. L. and J. R., two Georgia children. J. L. was born October 1963 and soon thereafter was adopted. When he was three, his parents were divorced and custody went to the mother; subsequently she remarried, gave birth to another child, and found herself having numerous problems with J. L. In 1970 she signed him into Central State Hospital as a voluntary patient. The staff doctors did not believe that J. L. required long-term inpatient care but could not arrange community placement. Hence he remained in Central State.

The second plaintiff, J. R., was removed from his natural parents at three months of age because of severe neglect. Over the next seven years, he moved through seven foster-home placements, and in 1970, when he was eight, the Georgia Department of Family and Children Services, his legal guardian, brought him to Central State Hospital. Its psychiatrists diagnosed him as borderline mentally retarded with "unsocialized aggressive reaction of childhood," and the state agency committed him to the facility as a voluntary patient. With J. R., as with J. L., the hospital staff soon preferred a community placement, but the state agency was unable to arrange it. Thus he too remained at Central State.

In 1975, attorneys from public-interest law firms brought a federal suit to win the release of the two children. They contended not only that J. L. and J. R. were entitled to services in the least restrictive alternative but that their original "voluntary" commitment was invalid. Hospitalization involved so massive a deprivation of liberty that neither a parent nor the state could act in proxy for the child. The child had a right to due

process before commitment, including the appointment of independent counsel to protect his interests.

The federal district court agreed. Hospitalization did
represent a fundamental loss of liberty ("the freedom to
go in and out the door, to go to school, and to frolic with
schoolmates"), and so commitment procedures had to
include due process. "Procedural safeguards" must
ensure "that even parents do not use the power to
indefinitely hospitalize children in an arbitrary manner." And what was true when parents acted was even
more true when the state, as guardian, moved for commitment. Nor was the district court satisfied merely
because psychiatrists had to approve the commitment
decisions: "Psychiatrists, like parents, cannot statuto-
rily be given the power to confine a child in a mental
hospital without procedural safeguards being imposed
to guard against errors in judgment." In sum, the decision represented a victory for the rights of mental
patients against psychiatrists, and even more dramatically, for the rights of children against parents.

The state of Georgia appealed all the way to the
United States Supreme Court, and won. The majority
opinion, rejecting each of the lower court's arguments,
ruled that due-process procedures were not required
in the commitment of children. "Although we acknowledge the fallibility of medical and psychiatric diag-
nosis," wrote Chief Justice Warren Burger for the
Court, "we do not accept the notion that the shortcom-
ings of specialists can always be avoided by shifting the
decision ... to an untrained judge." More, the state
could be allowed such power; it had a clear financial
interest in not committing its wards since hospital facilities were so very expensive. Finally, the Court insisted
that parents could be fully trusted to act in the best
interest of their children. The "natural bonds of affection" between parents and children justified this exercise of authority.

Parham is remarkable for its outright opposition to the most fundamental precepts of several rights movements. It summarily affirms the prerogatives of state officials, institutional psychiatrists, and parents and then goes on to dismiss both the usefulness and the propriety of adversarial procedures. It clarifies just how interconnected these various points are—how the support of the discretionary authority of one actor (the state or the expert) is linked to the support of the discretion of another (the parent), and how such a perspective is immediately antagonistic to litigation and a liberty model. More, *Parham* reveals the depth of the antagonism. As rights proponents see it, the Court fails to understand that considerations of power as well as sentiment often dictate parental choices, that decisions legitimated in the name of the best interest of the child may only be serving the best interest of the parent. Worse yet, for the Court to treat the state as though it were a parent, to allow a bureaucratic agency the same authority as a parent, is a throwback to the most naive of Progressive assumptions—the nightmare case, if you will, of paternalism cloaking oppression. Yet according to critics of the rights model, the Court acted wisely in not intruding into the realm of the family or challenging professional expertise. Parents and psychiatrists are far better equipped to protect the interests of the child than lawyers or judges through adversarial proceedings. In *Parham* the critics won, but it should be obvious from the character of the controversy that these issues will be repeatedly contested over the coming decade.

A third major battleground has emerged in the field of criminal justice and sentencing. The Progressive commitment to expanding administrators' authority, be they judges, probation officers, or parole officers, and to trusting in the rehabilitative potential of incarceration, whether in prisons or reformatories, did give way to an alternative view. The discretion of juvenile court judges seemed so unfettered that the Supreme Court, in the *Gault* decision, required the hearings to adhere to at least some procedural protections. Moreover, institutional conditions and practices seemed so offensive and substandard that federal courts frequently ruled some types of solitary confinement to be in violation of the Eighth Amendment ban on cruel and unusual punishment, or one or another prison rule to be an arbitrary and unreasonable limitation on prisoners. But again, as soon as one moved from the "easy" cases (easy in the sense that conditions were so horrific or regulations so absurd), agreement immediately broke down. Rights-minded activists, for example, urged the passage of fixed, determinate sentences which followed clear guidelines: so much punishment for so serious an offense. Initially, they found support among hard-line critics who believed that more mandatory sentencing policies would be tougher on the criminal. If those on the left of the political spectrum objected to sentences that ran three to ten years because the discretion of parole boards became the occasion for discrimination, with minorities serving closer to the ten than to the three, those on the right of the spectrum objected because the offenders were coddled, generally serving less than ten. It did not take long for the two sides to recognize that agreement on procedure, a commitment to determinate sentences, did not mean agreement on substance: the one group was looking to reduce time served; the other, to increase it.

To complicate matters further, a group still committed to Progressive principles has launched a staunch defense of indeterminate sentences. These traditional-minded liberals are repelled at the idea that anyone would dare to decide in advance how much punishment should be exacted of an offender; such a practice would rob criminal justice of every element of mercy, of all ability to respond to the special character of an individual case. Surely, it is relevant to the sentence that this offender is the product of an unfortunate upbringing, that that one had fallen on hard times, and so on. No matter how vigorously the critics of indeterminate sentences make their case, no matter what disparities in sentencing outcomes they cite, no matter how they prod their opponents to spell out mitigating circumstances that are constitutional or even fair, the opposition remains staunch, convinced that discretion in criminal justice benefits the offender.

The definition of constitutionally adequate institutional conditions is no less controversial than sentencing. Again, there was a brief period of agreement: no one doubted that the Arkansas prison's use of electric shock as an instrument of punishment was cruel and unusual, or that Texas's solitary cells were so bare and dark as to violate constitutional standards. Against such barbarisms, prisoners did have rights. But leave aside such barbarisms, and consensus disappears. In two recent Supreme Court decisions, the rights groups have suffered defeat. Is it cruel and unusual punishment to sentence a third-time felon (who has been convicted of three acts of grand larceny, but each of them for a paltry sum) to life imprisonment? The Court ruled that it is not. Is it a violation of the rights of accused persons awaiting trial for them to be confined two or more to a cell with little activity or exercise available? Once more, the Court ruled no. (Judge Rehnquist, writing for the majority, announced that he could find no principle of one man to one cell lurking in the Constitution.) Not that the prisoners' rights movement loses every case—there are sufficient nightmare situations in American prisons to preclude such an outcome—but the sense of momentum and opportunity for reform through litigation has been tempered. Each victory will now be hard-fought, and the casualties, in terms of cases lost, are bound to be high.

Perhaps the current intensity of the disputes and the speed with which counterreactions occurred indicate that from the start the alliance was not a very firm one. Psychiatrists or correctional administrators were never comfortable in the company of liberty-minded litigators. It was probably inevitable that the initial court decisions establishing one or another right would provoke a defensive reaction. No one likes being told how to run his affairs, especially if he has had eight years of postgraduate medical training or is fulfilling duties as complicated and problematic as running a prison. From the perspective of insiders, neither lawyers nor judges know much about treatment or about custody. Neither of them can appreciate the degree of illness in a mental patient or the degree of danger in a confined felon. Eavesdrop at a meeting of psychiatrists and you are bound to hear stories of a judge releasing a patient who then committed suicide. Go to a convention of wardens and you are bound to hear complaints that no one believes a felon who is on trial and protesting his innocence, but that everyone believes him once he is an inmate and protesting his conditions of incarceration.

Perhaps, too, mounting antagonisms were written into the script of the rights movement. The first victories of the litigators caught their opponents unprepared. For a moment, it was law-review graduates of the best Eastern institutions against run-of-the-mill attorneys in city or state legal offices. (If one goes to a convention of public-interest lawyers, one can hear such aphorisms as: Always sue the city on Friday and schedule your first court hearing for Monday, because no one who works for the city will work over the weekend.) But the situation has changed. Pushover victories are no longer to be had. Alabama and New York, for example, hire the best private lawyers (at taxpayers' expense, of course) to fight their fights. It was always implicit in the adversarial-rights model of social change that as one side armed, the other would also—and hence it would be naive to start complaining now that the shoot-out has begun.

But the matter goes deeper. Some of the first decisions promoting patients, rights did not unambiguously promote patients' well-being, not because the lawyers were heartless or the psychiatrists saboteurs, but rather because a mental health or a welfare system that for decades had been incapable of effectively serving clients was not about to be transformed overnight, or even over months or years. It was one thing for a court to order a change, quite another for a state bureaucracy to be able to effect the change—even assuming good will, which sometimes was and sometimes was not present. As a result, the failures continued—inmates remained unclothed in the institution or uncared for on the streets—supplying each side to the dispute with ample ammunition. In short order, every abuse uncovered in a community group home became the occasion for a psychiatrist to celebrate the virtues of the asylum. By the same token, the institution's ability to continue to dominate state departments of mental hygiene (so that dollars did not follow clients into the community) prompted attorneys to ponder where and how to file the next class-action lawsuit. All the while, the core of the problem remained with the immutable bureaucracy, with an inability to prod the slumbering giant to move, let alone to clean itself up.

Indeed, the more closely one examines the tangible effects of the litigators' first court victories, the more disappointing the results appear. The limits of court-ordered social change stand out starkly, not because litigators did not work hard enough or were too ambitious in their plans, but because legislators and administrators have been unwilling, and occasionally perhaps unable, to make the necessary commitments and investments. Yes, as Ira Glasser has noted, some boards of education now do follow formal procedures in disciplinary cases, but the number of school suspensions in many jurisdictions has increased because the core of the problem is untouched: that is, delivering meaningful education to inner-city children, teaching black children in ghetto schools in ways that will appear to be and prove to be useful. Yes, some state agencies do follow formal procedures before removing children from their natural or foster-care families, but many unnecessary removals continue to take place, again because the core of the problem is untouched: delivering meaningful social services and opportunities to lower-class families. Yes, the Supreme Court in *Donaldson* ruled that where a state hospital provides no treatment, a nondangerous mental patient cannot be deprived of his liberty. Nevertheless, very few inmates have been released under this ruling because of a failure to establish community residences and services. The list could be extended, but the point is already clear: the gap between courtroom victory and implementation looms so large that a disillusionment with the rights agenda even among its supporters is a very real prospect.

Bureaucratic resistance, maybe even immunity, to efforts at change is made all the worse by a severely shrinking economy. If it was still possible in the 1970s to retain some faint hopes for the promise of American life based on an expanding gross national product, a swelling fiscal pie, it is already a cliché in the early 1980s to think in terms of a zero-sum game. Whether the point at issue is how to control the rate of inflation or how to modernize American factories, it is clear that some groups are going to have to bear the burden more heavily than others. If federal spending is to be cut back in order to reduce inflation, the question is, from whose pocket will the sums come? Is it more likely that defense industries will suffer or health, education, and welfare programs? Will middle-class homeowners have to give up deducting mortgage interest payments or will lower-class recipients have to give up food stamps? Will the capital costs of reindustrialization go to shareholders or, through government write-offs, to taxpayers? In sum, there is every indication that public funds will get scarcer and scarcer and private interests will battle all the more fiercely to protect themselves. In such a situation, considerations of the social welfare of minorities have little prospect of being realized. We may well prove incapable of satisfying either rights or needs.

That so grim a forecast can become the occasion for jeremiads on narcissism almost defies imagination, whether they come from historians who substitute ideology for research and thought, or from presidents looking for scapegoats. The issues are not, in the end, moral issues, a text for sermons. As is almost always the case, diatribes against individual malfeasance are a poor substitute for a sustained analysis of the politics and the economics of the situation.

The implications of such a state of affairs for those who would try to set limits on benevolence and recast the definition of doing good are certainly not encouraging, but the record demonstrates that the rights movement is entering a second stage whose essential features, the more bitter ideological controversies and the more hard-fought court battles, should prompt a rethinking of strategies for change. Turning one's back on the rights principles, giving the professionals the discretion they are clamoring for, will not resolve the conflicts. To revive a Progressive outlook and policy in the 1980s would be an even more forlorn and hopeless task than it was in the 1970s. Efforts to win acceptance for a definition of the common weal, to think in terms of the good of all, when such terms as "reindustrialization," "deflation," and "zero-sum game" permeate our vocabulary, are bound to produce either platitudes or mischief. This is the moment not to abandon the idea of limiting discretion and expanding rights but rather to conceive of more appropriate strategies for accomplishing these ends. To win a big court victory in a class-action suit is no longer a sufficient ambition. Activists must begin to think about power in more complicated ways, to make sophisticated calculations about political leverage and constituent political groups. Courts and litigation will always remain vital to the movement, but it is also appropriate now to devote new attention to legislative and administrative concerns. To be sure, this is not a welcome assignment, not in principle and not in light of the record. To press minority interests before majority-minded legislatures or bureaucracies is, at the least, difficult, and may be doomed to failure. And yet, given the developments we have been tracing here, there may be little other choice, even as the nation's politics turns more conservative.

To draw out the implications of this position for the rights agenda, it is instructive to explore the attempt to monitor and reduce the discretion of research scientists through the mechanism of the Institutional Review Board. The IRB was very much the product of post-Progressive attitudes, a decline in trust in the expert, a loss of confidence in the idea that self-interest (of the researcher) and public interest (of the subject or of society) could coincide. New federal regulations required institutions to establish boards that would scrutinize research protocols and the procedures by which researchers obtained the "informed consent" of their subjects. The IRB was to serve as a watchdog committee to help make certain that experimentation on human subjects was not abusive or unethical. Although it is too soon to offer definitive judgments, the IRBs generally have not lived up to their mandate. Too much of their work is cursory. They lack the capacity to delve deeply into the issues that come before them, and they are woefully unable to monitor results or see to the implementation of their recommendations. Given these failures, one can hear all sorts of professionals calling for abandonment of the IRB. Ostensibly it is one more example of federal regulations senselessly constraining a vital activity.

But this record can better serve as a stimulus to think longer and harder about political leverage. Had the framers of IRB regulations done this, they would not have paid such scant attention to appointment procedures for board members, considerations of tenure, the balance of power on the committees, and so on. Under present rules, the very institution that is conducting the research is responsible for appointing IRB members, and nothing in the regulations prevents it from dismissing a dissident member, who might regularly protest poorly drawn or misleading consent forms, or packing the IRB with members far more eager to maximize the number of research grants to the institution than to minimize risk to research subjects. A sensitivity to political leverage makes the need for a wholesale reform of the IRB mechanism obvious. Otherwise, the regulations will not do much more than produce paper without affecting substance, and so fuel the movement for their elimination.

This same perspective brought to bear on deinstitutionalization might encourage the movement to locate and build up constituent groups whose political power would be exercised on behalf of community services. At the moment, the politics all run in one direction, in favor of the institution. Think of construction contractors; legislators who curry favor with property owners determined to exclude group homes from their neigh-

borhoods; union leaders whose members work in institutions and are worried about their jobs; the institutional superintendents ready to defend their fiefdoms
by any and all tactics. Who stands on the other side? A
few disgruntled parents of residents, a handful of litigators and academics, a neighborhood church that rents
out its basement for a day program. Could one create a
constituency for deinstitutionalization? This is the right
question, and there are reasons to answer it positively.
It is possible to make alliances with large voluntary
agencies, who are sure to extract a price of their own (in
terms of service contracts), but the price might well be
worth paying. One can find landlords eager to rent a
number of apartments. It is simple to have group
homes shop locally and not be supplied from a central
depot, so that the grocer, butcher, and baker enjoy
their business. To be sure, imbalances in power will
remain. Construction contractors support election
campaigns more generously than small merchants.
Nevertheless, such an effort at coalition-building might
begin to alter the balance. A court decree *and* a political constituency might be able to accomplish something together that neither can do separately.

For those who doubt the significance of thinking in
terms of adversarial procedures and rights, the outcome in the *Parham* case warrants another look. The
Court's refusal to limit the discretionary authority of
professionals, administrators, and parents to commit a
child to a state mental hospital demonstrates all too viv-
idly the disadvantages of ignoring considerations of
power. *Parham*, it should be said, is not an easy case for
rights advocates, and yet, even here, inattention to
their principles has unfortunate results. It is true that
enhancing the authority of the child against the parent
raises the prospect of enhancing the authority of the
state against the family. In practical terms, it would be a
public agency that typically enforced the right of the

child against the parent—and the potential for abuse in such a situation is considerable. Any one parent can do mischief only on a small scale; the state can do harm on a large scale. Hence, where a family is intact and functioning, it would be inappropriate to introduce procedures or parties that would coerce the parents. As long as a parent is fulfilling his or her responsibilities in lawful fashion, so that neglect or abuse is not at issue, the rights of the child ought not to be established through the exercise of state power. However, as soon as parents begin to neglect their responsibilities in child care, as soon as the wall around the family shows signs of crumbling, then it becomes critical to expand children's rights, to provide them with lawyers and advocates, and to afford them procedural protection against the abuse of authority.

Parham demonstrates the value of this principle. For one, it establishes that the state should not enjoy the same rights as parents to commit a child to an institution. Just as the child, without danger to the integrity of the family, can exercise rights against schools, so too he ought to be able to exercise rights against a mental hospital. For another, it demonstrates that in this instance, parental authority ought to be curtailed. In committing a child to an institution, the family is clearly loosening, if not surrendering, its control over the child, and at just this point, considerations of power are far more relevant than considerations of sentiment. More, in this case giving the child independent counsel does not in itself undermine family integrity. The state is already deeply involved, and even the most adversarial commitment contest, with parents and lawyers lined up on one side and child and lawyers on the other, does little worse than remind parents just how drastic a step commitment is (if commitment is appropriate). Of course, if a court finds that commitment is inappropriate, then the parents may have a burden to bear, but the child will have been spared an exceptionally drastic fate.

Finally, allowing the child independent counsel in *Parham* might have expanded the rights of the child without undercutting parental authority at all. The Central State psychiatrists were prepared to discharge both J. L. and J. R. but could find no place other than the hospital's wards for treatment. At an adversarial hearing, the focus need not have been on the rights of the parent versus those of the child, but on the right of the child to receive services in the least restrictive setting. The child's advocate might have persuaded the court to compel the state to establish community services, in this way securing the rights of the child against the state. In sum, *Parham* might have served the family well if it had looked to power, not to sentiment.

The effort to realize rights and needs, to win the courtroom victory and carry it through to implementation, has nowhere taken on a more dramatic quality than in the deinstitutionalization of Willowbrook. In the spring of 1975, New York State signed a consent decree promising to phase down Willowbrook over the next six years and return its 5,200 mentally retarded inmates to residences in the community. For Sheila Rothman and for me, this massive state commitment provided a superb test case for evaluating court-ordered social change, for reckoning with the possibilities of reform through litigation, for analyzing whether social service systems can be transformed in novel ways. A full account of our research will soon appear, but some preliminary statements on this attempt to do good are appropriate here.

In 1972, Willowbrook was a hellhole. Everyone was embarrassed at the snakepit-like conditions, and first-stage consensus was not difficult to achieve. Willowbrook would have to be cleaned up; every reputable professional agreed. Indeed, the consent decree of 1975 spelled out in exquisite detail the services that

New York pledged to provide. Most of the specifics were aimed at improving the quality of life within the institution (so many staff, so many hours of programs). But at the same time, the decree ordered community placement, the provision of the least restrictive alternative for all of the residents.

The stage-one agenda, cleaning up the institution, was never especially controversial. The litigators for the Willowbrook class and the court-appointed monitors—the Willowbrook Review Panel—were not, and still are not, altogether content with the progress made in the buildings; shortages of clothing and of staff can still be found on occasion. But no one doubts that Willowbrook today is a far cry from Willowbrook in 1972. There is a medical program, there are teachers, there are screens on the windows, the toilets generally flush, staff ratios are much improved. Probably the critical element underlying this progress is that the number of residents has been greatly reduced, from 5,200 to some 1,500 (as of the fall of 1980).

But it is precisely this drop in population, the community-placement effort, that has been the most difficult to achieve and most often the occasion for charges, countercharges, litigation, conflict, and altogether adversarial relationships. This stage-two enterprise, the actual implementation of the court order, the return of the residents to the community, reveals both the promise and the problems in such a program. Once the retarded had left their traditional place inside the institution, protest came from almost every quarter. Community planning boards passed resolutions against locating a group home in their midst. Some parents vehemently objected to their children leaving Willowbrook; however grim the conditions, the place had a stability about it which was not immediately apparent to them in a group home. State agencies balked at the paperwork, at carrying out the necessary architectural revisions. The public schools were reluctant to provide former inmates with classrooms and teachers, a reluctance that turned into hysteria when some of the would-be students were diagnosed as silent carriers of hepatitis B. And not surprisingly, the State Office of Mental Retardation could not keep up a steady pace of placements, to the disappointment of the Review Panel and the plaintiff lawyers—who had the state back in court on a regular basis.

Nevertheless, for all the conflict, the accomplishments have been considerable. The court case has acted as a catalyst for change, helping to create the conditions and even the constituents for deinstitutionalization that were simply not to be found in 1975. Some 1,500 members of the Willowbrook class are now in group homes, almost all of which are decent and well run; the clients are receiving a minimum of six hours of programs a day and a good deal of recreational services in addition. (Some of the homes, let it be said, are exemplary and only a few of them are problematic.) The lawyers have proved themselves fully capable of devoting as much attention to needs as to rights, and the state bureaucracy, however haltingly and spasmodically, has been able to implement a community program. Perhaps even more encouraging, something of a constituency for deinstitutionalization is being created after the fact. When parents visit the group homes, their opposition generally fades; they know a quality program when they see one in operation. Community protest also disappears once a group home is functioning; within six months of its opening, the group home is no longer the focus of agitation. Even the schools are adjusting. It turns out that many of the retarded can be taught, that hepatitis B carriers are not a source of contagion in a classroom. Finally, the state has contracted with many private, not-for-profit agencies to deliver services to the Willowbrook class; these agencies are now beginning to have something of a stake in community-based programs, and may actually exercise some political influence on their behalf.

None of this should be taken to mean that the Willowbrook effort is now nearly complete, quietly in place, and smoothly functioning. The great majority of clients are still in institutions—if not in Willowbrook itself, then in other 300-bed to 500-bed facilities. It is still not clear whether the State Office of Mental Retardation has a system in place or is just managing to respond on a daily basis to one or another crisis. Community planning boards still fight the new group home; the Review Panel has many more enemies than friends (indeed, the legislature just canceled its funding). Relationships among the several parties are anything but cordial, and it is not yet apparent whether a monitoring system that will protect the needs and rights of clients is firmly in place. The final verdict on the outcome remains to be delivered. The only appropriate conclusion here is that meaningful social change through a court action is possible. The effort to promote the rights of the Willowbrook class has served the needs of many of them quite well, at least to this moment.

In sum, reviewing the argument of *Doing Good* is chastening and makes clear, sometimes painfully clear, that the matter of benevolence is still conflict-ridden. Nevertheless, the prospects are not as bleak as one might fear. Recent developments not only make apparent that the questions raised in these essays are the central questions to confront, but that the answers suggested here, an appreciation of the values of a liberty model and an adversarial approach, continue to point social thought and social policy in the right direction.

D. J. R.
New York City
November, 1980

About the Authors

WILLARD GAYLIN, a practicing psychoanalyst and psychiatrist, is the co-founder and president of the Institute of Society, Ethics and and the Life Sciences, as well as the author of some nine books, the most recent of which is *Feelings*.

IRA GLASSER, currently executive director of the American Civil Liberties Union, began his career in social work for the blind, taught mathematics at several universities, was the editor of *Current* magazine, and has contributed extensively to books and journals.

STEVEN MARCUS, formerly director of planning for the National Humanities Center, is a Rockefeller Foundation Fellow in the Humanities for 1980–81, and is the author of four books, the most recent of which is *Representations: Essays on Literature and Society*.

DAVID J. ROTHMAN is a professor of history at Columbia University and the initiator of this volume. His most recent book is *Conscience and Convenience: The Asylum and Its Alternatives in Progressive America*.